Symposium on Consciousness

Symposium on Consciousness

Presented at the annual meeting of
the American Association for
the Advancement of Science
February 1974

PHILIP R. LEE

ROBERT E. ORNSTEIN

DAVID GALIN

ARTHUR DEIKMAN

CHARLES T. TART

The Viking Press | *New York*

First published in 1976 by The Viking Press, Inc. 625 Madison Avenue, New York, N.Y. 10022

Published simultaneously in Canada by The Macmillan Company of Canada Limited

LIBRARY OF CONGRESS CATALOGING IN PUBLICATION DATA

Symposium on Consciousness, San Francisco, 1974.
    Symposium on Consciousness.

    Includes bibliographical references.
    1. Consciousness—Congresses. I. Lee, Philip R. II. American Association for the Advancement of Science.
BF311.S845   1974   153   75-30642
ISBN   0-670-68903-3

Printed in U.S.A.

Acknowledgment is made to the following: Collins-Knowlton-Wing, Inc., for material from *The Exploits of the Incomparable Mulla Nasrudin* by Idries Shah. Copyright © 1966 by Mulla Nasrudin Enterprises Ltd. Collins-Knowlton-Wing, Inc., and A. P. Watt & Son, for material from *Caravan of Dreams* by Idries Shah. Copyright © 1968 by Idries Shah. Reprinted by permission.

Note

The symposium was conceived and arranged by
Philip R. Lee and Robert E. Ornstein,
the book by Robert E. Ornstein,
in conjunction with the
Institute for the Study of Human Knowledge.

Contents

Symposium on Consciousness

1 PHILIP R. LEE, M. D. AND FRANCES PETROCELLI

Can Consciousness Make a Difference?

More than eight hundred people attended the Symposium on Consciousness at the 1974 Annual Meeting of the American Association for the Advancement of Science (AAAS), making it one of the largest gatherings at the meeting. This interest, in some ways unanticipated, was a reflection of the growing concern of social, behavioral, and medical scientists, as well as of the general public, about the development of a more adequate and comprehensive understanding of human consciousness.

This symposium was not the first effort of the AAAS to explore human consciousness. It is particularly appropriate for this interdisciplinary scientific organization to engage in these discussions. In the last decade, a variety of disciplines, including bioengineering, physics, anthropology, psychology, psychiatry, neurology, neurophysiology, and biochemistry, have been in the forefront of research that has increased our knowledge of human consciousness, altered states of awareness, and mind-body relationships.

In this paper I do not discuss in any detail the material

that was presented and discussed in the symposium. My goal is to place the symposium in a larger context by discussing other ideas in the field and then discussing some areas of personal interest that complement the topics covered.

In the AAAS symposium, it was possible to deal in depth with only a few of the ideas that have begun to be explored in the area of consciousness. But Drs. Ornstein, Galin, Deikman, and Tart, in dealing with the brain and conscious experiences, have, I believe, begun to bridge the gap between Western understanding of what many call "intuitive knowledge" and scientific observation. They emphasized the different functions of the two hemispheres of the brain, psychophysiological studies of consciousness, and what Tart calls "discrete states of consciousness." Both Deikman and Ornstein related these to "esoteric" Eastern psychologies and mystic experiences.

My view of human consciousness reflects my background in medicine and my interest in health as well as disease. It has been my experience that to the degree that I am aware of my own consciousness or reality, I can recognize and respond to that of others. It is possible that an understanding of consciousness can have as great an impact on health as have some of the scientific advances in medical care. Medicine's focus, in fact, has been on disease, not health. But doctors know that health is affected by biology, behavior, the environment, and education to a greater extent than it is affected by medical care. I would place consciousness at the head of this list because if consciousness is recognition of the fact that there is an inner being who knows what is real, and who is in charge of the organism and what happens, then increased awareness of this may make health become a reality.

I will begin with a consideration of how different disciplines view reality and human consciousness, move on to recent developments in the area of mind-body relationships, discuss holistic approaches to medicine as a practical application of some of these changing ideas, consider the need for humanization in medicine and in education, and conclude with some thoughts on the possible implications of the evolution of human consciousness.

SEVERAL VIEWS OF REALITY

Interest in human consciousness is widespread throughout our society and is reflected both in the research and general interest in such diverse fields and activities as meditation, biofeedback, altered states of awareness, and awareness training, Eastern religions, "mind-expanding" drugs, parapsychology, and esoteric psychologies. In fields as diverse as physics and religion, neurophysiology and anthropology, philosophy and clinical medicine, ideas once thought to be alien or incomprehensible are now the subject of serious inquiry. A variety of groups, ranging from small religious sects, to awareness-training organizations, to new professional societies and university-based research groups, have been organized in an effort to understand and to bring together in a coherent way the mystical visions of reality of the East and the rational, objective view of reality of the West.

This is an era of great change in science, including those disciplines that deal with the subjective, inner experiences. Scientists are acknowledging that there is more to scientific investigation than has been discussed. Indeed, the scientific view of reality is itself being explored. It has been pointed out by educator Willis Harman that "since we have come to understand that science is not a description of 'reality' but a metaphorical ordering of experience, the new science does not impugn the old. It is not a question of which view is 'true' in some ultimate sense. Rather, it is a matter of which picture is more useful in guiding human affairs."[1]

In discussing perceptions of reality, Lawrence LeShan, a psychologist, differentiates between "commonsense" reality (the individual reality used in everyday life in Western society), "scientific" reality (the individual reality of modern physics), and "mystical" reality. He uses the term "individual reality" to "denote those aspects of reality which the individual perceives, responds to, or interacts with."[2] Westerners have accepted the commonsense and scientific individual realities but have not really acknowledged the striking differences in approach between the two. The scientific reality represents an approach just as different from common-sense reality as mystical reality because it is not perceived through the senses.

Dr. LeShan discusses the physicist's view and the mystic's view of reality and notes: "Both mystic and physicist are trying to build a *better* (more accurate for his purposes) picture of how the cosmos works. One rejects his senses as a path to this understanding; the other rejects the evidence of his senses."[3] Although the physicist and the mystic differ radically in their approaches, LeShan believes they agree in their attempts to understand reality.

Few have described the problems or the possibilities of our perceptions of reality more clearly than the physicist John Wheeler:

> Insofar as we've learned to understand the quantum principle, it's the small tip of an iceberg that tells us that the momentum and the position of the electron are not qualities that exist independently of us but depend upon our consciously making a decision to measure the position and the momentum in order to bring these features into evidence. I think that through our act of consciously choosing and posing questions about the universe we bring about in some measure what we see taking place before us.

He went on:

> Therefore, I think the word "observing" is inadequate. A better word is "participation." We are going to come to appreci-

ate that the universe itself in some strange way depends on our being here for its properties. "Depends" is perhaps not the right word, because it implies that the universe is dependent upon us, when there is a mutuality of relationship that needs to be stated.[4]

It is interesting, and perhaps startling, to find that John Wheeler's ideas about "participation" are not so different from the findings of Carlos Castaneda in his journeys with the Mexican Indian sorcerer don Juan. Castaneda, an anthropologist, found that his perceptions of reality were often only his perceptions and that to experience don Juan's world of nonordinary reality, he was forced to suspend his rational judgment and his cultural attitudes—and participate in don Juan's world. Don Juan says to his pupil, "There are lots of things that you do now which would have seemed insane to you ten years ago. Those things themselves did not change, but your idea of yourself changed; what was impossible before is perfectly possible now, and perhaps your total success in changing yourself is only a matter of time."[5]

Castaneda, in his descriptions of the teachings of don Juan, has made it easier for the Western mind to see that there are different realities as well as different levels of awareness of those realities.

Perhaps the most exciting fields of potential research in relation to human consciousness are psychology, physics, and physiology, particularly neurophysiology. Why has it taken these disciplines so long to explore areas of great importance related to human consciousness? William James, before the turn of the century, pointed the way to many of the current scientific explorations:

> Our normal waking consciousness, rational consciousness as we call it, is but one special type of consciousness, whilst all about it, parted from it by the filmiest of screens, there lie potential forms of consciousness entirely different. We may go through

life suspecting their existence, but apply the requisite stimulus and at a touch they are there in all their completeness, definite types of mentality which probably somewhere have their field of application and adaptation.[6]

Being able to look at reality in a different way may seem difficult. But science has changed before. In the seventeenth century, science was revolutionized by a conceptual shift from the qualitative aspects of properties to the quantitative mathematics of measurables. A science of consciousness, or of ways of knowing, may also require a conceptual revolution.

RECENT DEVELOPMENTS IN MIND-BODY RELATIONSHIPS

One potentially revolutionary development in the field of human consciousness has been in mind-body relationships. Although this subject has long been of interest to psychologists, physiologists, physicians, and philosophers, many conceptual and methodological barriers have impeded the development of a better understanding. A major barrier has been the approach of Western scientists and physicians, who have been unable to acknowledge the potential of human consciousness because of their limited view of reality. Dr. Ornstein has observed that our rational, linear, analytic mode of investigation and thinking has "prevented us from clearly seeing the scientific impact of the esoteric traditions. For hundreds of years reports have reached the West of yogis who could stop their hearts and alter their glandular and metabolic activity. But since we consider such control impossible, we have almost completely ignored these fragmentary communications."[7] This ignorance is rapidly being dispelled in research laboratories in many parts of the world.

Biofeedback research is one of the facets of this expanded interest in the "irrelevant" and the "impossible." The concept of biofeedback is that body processes produce specific effects on the brain. By a mechanism not yet understood, it is possible for the human being to produce controlled effects on the body that can be measured by electronic sensors and reported by a variety of measuring devices. Its potential impact on psychology, medicine, biomedical research, and human health is beginning to be explored. Hypertension, arrhythmias, and other cardiovascular disturbances as well as muscular and gastrointestinal malfunctions may be ameliorated in whole or in part by the conscious control of autonomic functions which seems to be possible once the mind has read the indicators. Psychosomatic illnesses may, at long last, be treated effectively. In a recent adaptation of her book, *New Mind, New Body*, Dr. Barbara Brown noted:

> The importance of these studies to medicine is enormous. Psychosomatic illness affects great segments of our society, yet some illnesses are among the most difficult to diagnose and to treat. What the work of Mill and his colleagues implies is that something in the brain, the mind or the will can be just as effective in relieving illnesses as it is in causing illnesses. More important, their work and that of others even suggests that the will can affect, and perhaps correct, disease processes of largely organic origins. The greater understanding of the relationship between brain and body, the more this understanding can lead to effective use of medicine and psychological tools.[8]

Medicine is not the only health profession which may benefit greatly from some of the recent developments in the study of mind-body relationships. In physical therapy, for example, the relation of the mind and body has received renewed attention. One outcome has been the development of Structural Integration, a technique of physical therapy which deals with the alignment of an individual's body in the gravitational field. Developed by a biochemist, Dr. Ida Rolf, Structural Integration also deals very directly with the relationship of the body to the mind and the mind to the body. Anyone who has had the personal experience of being

"Rolfed" can describe the emotional release that may occur, the flashes of memory that bring both old and long-forgotten experiences to consciousness, and the influence of emotional resistance to the feeling of pain during treatment.

The concept of Structural Integration is based on the premises that, first, our bodies are material objects in a three-dimensional world and are subject to the laws of mechanics; and, second, our bodies are plastic and capable of change. Underlying these premises is the view that gravity can influence not only man's physical structure but also his vitality and well-being. It is the goal of Structural Integration to realign the plastic structure of the body so that the energy field of gravity can act to support the energy field of man.[9]

The effects of Structural Integration as presently practiced are beginning to be studied in an objective fashion. Studies include measurement of biochemical, electromyographic, and electroencephalographic changes before, during, and after ten hour-long sessions of Structural Integration manipulation or massage. These studies, like others attempting to relate the effects of body states to consciousness, are still experimental and relatively elementary.

Even a brief review of recent developments related to human consciousness demands some discussion of the growth of the awareness-training groups. It began in the early 1960s with the Esalen Institute. President Richard Farson describes Esalen's efforts this way: "It seems to me that what Esalen does best is to make the invisible visible, whether it is a hidden personal feeling, a strongly defended unconscious process, a covert interpersonal style, a higher form of consciousness or a new dimension of awareness."[10] Other organizations, such as est, Arica, Transcendental Meditation, Claudio Naranjo's groups, and the Zen and yoga groups, have also been concerned with providing the means for individuals to experience themselves as being aware, living in the present and in control of their lives. Large numbers of people have participated in various of these programs.

It has been empirically observed in follow-up studies that some individuals who have participated in programs of consciousness or awareness training and meditation have been able to reduce or eliminate their use of "mind-expanding" drugs, tranquilizers, or analgesic drugs. Many individuals have also been able to reduce markedly or stop smoking cigarettes. These results can clearly promote increased health and well-being, even though "health" is not the purpose of these training programs—they do not stress or even mention reduction in drug or cigarette use.

Many clinical psychologists and psychotherapists are also being influenced by the growing awareness of consciousness and the techniques developed to experience consciousness. Carl Rogers' client-centered approach and Abraham Maslow's theories about the healthy personality contributed to the challenge to psychoanalysis several years ago. There was also Fritz Perls's development of Gestalt therapy. Now there are the myriad other recent developments. As consciousness or self-awareness becomes better understood and accepted, I believe that more and more therapies involving individuals, families, or other groups will be adapted to take advantage of this new knowledge.

A word of caution: It is essential that ethical interest and objective inquiry in any of these areas not be replaced by fadism and exploitation. Medicine is subject to fads and quackery, particularly where the emotions or the mind are involved. This has, regrettably, long been true even within the mainstream of medical science and medical care. As an example, from the mid- to the late-nineteenth century, the uterus and the ovaries were thought to play the dominant role in women's illnesses. The philosophy was that female psychology functioned merely as an extension of female reproductivity, and that woman's nature was determined by her reproductive functions. This led to a host of bizarre and brutal therapies, none more outrageous than the removal of normal ovaries. The indications for this procedure included "troublesomeness, eating like a ploughman, masturbation, attempted suicide, erotic tendencies, persecution mania, simple cussedness, and dysmenorrhea. Most apparent in the enormous variety of symptoms doctors took to indicate castration was a strong current of sexual appetitiveness on the part of women."[11]

Nor have fads in medicine in the last century been limited to surgical procedures and diseases thought to be characteristic of women. Medicines, whether prescribed or purchased over-the-counter, have long been subject to misuse or irrational use based on false hopes and misleading promotional practices. For example, in modern times treatment of emotional problems and mental illness has been the subject of changing fashions. Sedatives, particularly barbiturates, were touted as the answer in the 1940s; amphetamines and other pep pills in the 1950s; tranquilizers in the 1960s; and, now, in the 1970s, antidepressants are promoted as the solution for depression, which is being called our most common unrecognized illness.

Biofeedback, meditation, awareness training, and other approaches are all subject to false claims, excessive or overzealous promotion, and other abuses in a society that is as puzzled and perplexed as our own. These hazards can be mitigated, however, by sound research and an adequate and realistic public-education effort.

HOLISTIC APPROACHES TO MEDICINE

Meditation, manipulation, massage, and biofeedback all seem to fit into a broader context of mind-body relationship that is altering our past views. David Sobel recently observed: "Any process which organizes and patterns the nervous system and the body, whether by mantras, mandalas, rhythmic breathing exercises, stroboscopes, dervish dancing, yogic postures or Structural Integration, is likely to affect the consciousness of man."[12]

One of the most important outcomes of these recent developments, whether brain research, biofeedback, Structural Integration, or the awareness-training efforts, is a renewed interest in health and the responsibility of the individual for his own health. As medicine has become more and more scientific, and medical care more and more technologically dependent, the burden of responsibility has shifted increasingly from the patient to the physician. We are now learning, through a better understanding of the mind-body relationship, that there is more the individual can do, not only to ameliorate signs and symptoms of disease but to fashion a state of physical and mental health and well-being. This includes not only such obvious care for oneself as not smoking but also greater concern with proper nutrition, exercise, relaxation, and the relationship of the body to the forces of gravity.

Holistic approaches to medicine focus on the promotion of health and well-being, on the self-awareness of the individual, and on the prevention of disease. They relate to the whole person and are based on a synthesis of Western medicine and traditional systems of medicine. Their development and acceptance are potentially very important outgrowths of our new knowledge and openness to ideas that, at best, seemed distant or alien only a few years ago.

Mind-body relationships have been approached very differently in the medical care systems of other cultures. These differences reflect cultural differences and entirely different ways of viewing the reality of man. These are not competing systems because they are not scientific in Western terms. Perhaps we can accept them as complementary ways of viewing man, just as various scientific disciplines look at man very differently.

Chinese traditional medicine, yogic therapy, and the medicine of American Indians are all conceptually different, and they all differ radically from modern, scientific Western medicine. In spite of these differences, there may be a great deal to learn from these dissimilar approaches.

During a visit to the People's Republic of China in 1973, I saw traditional and Western medicine being blended after years of conflict and confrontation. Efforts are being made to understand better the conceptual basis of many of the traditional therapies, such as acupuncture, which was rejected in China by virtually all Western-trained physicians until the past decade.

The basis of Chinese traditional medicine is unusual by Western terms. It is founded on the view that man is a microcosm of the universe and subject to the same disruptions as nature itself. It stresses that disease is not a localized process but is the result of being out of balance and not adhering to the Tao, the immutable course of nature. Although the concepts of the opposing and unifying forces of Yin and Yang have no scientific basis, the clinical approach of the traditional practitioners has gained increased acceptance because some of their methods, such as acupuncture, have been found empirically to be useful in specific situations. Traditional Chinese therapy, in addition to acupuncture, includes moxibustion, massage, physical exercises, and dietary regimens. With the exception of moxibustion, all of these have attracted renewed interest among many Western-trained physicians throughout the world.

How is Chinese traditional medicine related to the psychology of human consciousness or to our own efforts in health? This is not an easy question to answer, but because of the Chinese holistic view of man and the relationship of mind and body, I think we will find observations which are important to our concepts of health and disease, and to our treatment of people with a variety of diseases.

In our own country, Dr. Harold Wise, a pioneer in social medicine and health care for the poor, is establishing with his colleagues a Center for Holistic Medicine in New York City.

The program will be "dedicated to working on the whole health of a community of 200 families, bringing physical skill to illness, psychological skill to distress, and human concern to the process of people becoming more fully functioning. Its staff of traditional therapists will be committed to helping the center's clients unfold their own strengths to prevent, resist, and recover from disease, to confront normal crisis in their personal development, and grow as parents, as people working and as individuals living together."[13] A number of other groups have begun similar efforts, some focusing on the training of health professionals to learn these new approaches while others have focused on individual patients in the health-care system.

The importance of individual or psychological factors in maintaining health and facilitating the healing process is increasingly being understood. The psychological approach when incorporated within a holistic system may yield more effective ways of dealing with health problems than the current approaches, which emphasize drug therapies.

HUMANIZATION IN MEDICINE AND EDUCATION

The pioneering approaches in holistic medicine are paralleled by a variety of efforts to humanize health care. At the heart of attempts at humanization are our image of man, how we value man, and how we treat the individual. Is the individual seen as a person who feels, who has intelligence, who cares, and who has an inalienable right to choose how he or she will live, learn, and even die? Or have the human qualities become secondary in our rush toward those elements that can be measured by machines? I believe that the reliance on machines has come about partly because of the Westerner's inability to be in touch with consciousness. Physicians and patients alike have suffered from the inability to communicate with each other from their experience of themselves and from their experience of the other person.

In the United States, the technological approach to health has reached its peak in coronary intensive-care units, kidney-dialysis centers, and cardiovascular surgery theaters with heart-lung machines, cardiac bypasses, and other miracles of modern science and technology. Too often the patient has been ignored and physiological functions stressed instead. Patients often feel that the monitoring and support machines have, in fact, taken over. When this happens, the result is depersonalized and dehumanized health care. Investigators are finding that in some situations people do not respond physically because the human element has not been considered. A new look has to be taken at the human being's reality in these situations.

Dehumanization has become apparent in other areas. Consider our approach to death. Death has long been viewed as the archenemy of medicine, to be fought with every weapon, postponed and delayed, although never defeated. Increasingly, patients have been hospitalized and kept alive, or their deaths delayed, by the use of modern technology, including drugs, intravenous fluids, injections, and respirators. Who is being kept alive and for what are forgotten in the battle.

The medical approach, of course, is not an isolated one. The view of death that has evolved in our society is one of fear and abhorrence of the unnatural. In fact, what is more natural than birth and then death? The emphasis on youth, production, and impersonal ways of living has contributed to this phenomenon. The celebration of life and the inability to face death have been reflected in such things as high-priced, unrealistic, and exotic funerals in America, as dramatically discussed by Jessica Mitford in *The American Way of Death*.

But things are beginning to change. A recent review in *The New York Times* discussed several books on death and dying—all of which look at Western attitudes on death.[14] The books are about people dying, about those who are with them during the process, and some are written by people who are in the process. Many dealing directly with the subject of death have come to the view that their essentiality continues after death as we know it.

Regardless of the individual's view of what comes before—or after—the ability to accept death as part of life is extremely important. With more and more people beginning to discuss and study the subject of death, perhaps we can gain some insight into why those in the esoteric traditions ask us to think about death. It is far more human to acknowledge and deal with our true feelings about it than to refuse to face whatever the reality is.

Studies have shown that educated people are healthier people and that, in fact, education may be more important in relation to health than the availability of medical care. Just as with health care, education is now seen by many as needing to be humanized. By this I mean creating an atmosphere in which each child's individual human qualities can unfold and be nurtured, and in which the individual's ability to be responsible for his or her own learning is realized.

Most of us have models of behavior or of development for children. A great many of these models are built on the assumption that you have to *do* something to the child for his or her development to be positive. In other words, stated in an exaggerated fashion, the child is viewed as a machine which has to be programed. In this model, which fits our technological approach, parents and teachers view their roles as molding or conditioning the child's behavior. Werner Erhard, the founder of est, an awareness-training organization which also provides training for children, says that "education was intended to elevate people's well being but there is no evidence that it has been able to do this. The educated are not better off beings because of their education. It is true that they have more information which allows them to pursue different kinds of lives than the uneducated pursue. They have the symbols of being educated but do not necessarily experience themselves as knowing beings. What is needed is a system that allows people to experience themselves as being intelligent, able, aware, knowing and able to communicate effectively."[15]

Much of the research in the consciousness area has the potential for affecting our ability to communicate. Since education is communication, this new knowledge may contribute to the humanization of the educational process and the growth of the individuals involved.

Recognizing that the child is a whole person who, like the adult, feels, sees, thinks, and has his or her own reality will facilitate the learning process. The ability to relate to individual differences was referred to by Idries Shah, the leader of the Sufis, when he said, "Please do not start to teach the blind until you have practiced living with closed eyes."[16]

If the educational process can recognize the uniqueness and the value of each child, it may become even more important in the development of healthy human beings.

Implications

What does this all mean? If consciousness is, as I believe, recognition of the fact that there is an inner being who knows what is real, and who is in charge of the organism and what happens, does it mean that we are beings whose reality is in fact created or given form by our consciousness? What are the implications of some of the findings in the consciousness area? Some of the implications may be that our existing institutions, like medicine and education, will begin to work as we begin to understand where the responsibility for these institutions lies.

The renowned biologist Salvador E. Luria talks about a "biology of the human spirit," and suggests that the evolution of the human mind may have been a correlate of the development of language. Dr. Luria says: "Some may believe that a biology of the mind is impossible, either on theological or on philosophical grounds. I take here a different view, that a biology of the mind is feasible and is one of the great goals of science, possibly the greatest."[17]

I will take that one step farther and say that perhaps the human race has developed to a point where it is ready for the realization of human consciousness. We may say, "What difference does it make? Man cannot change." But it may be that man doesn't need to change. It may be, instead, that if it is possible for man to become aware of what and who he is, we will be able to realize a better world. This better world would preclude the persistent pursuit of the belief that man is essentially a machine whose behavior ultimately can be controlled. Many involved in the study of consciousness have come to know that consciousness cannot be manipulated. The unconscious processes which prevent us from experiencing consciousness can be, however. In fact, psychologists have long known that the unconscious processes are automatic or machinelike in their nature. Much of our society, as is evident in advertising and the manipulation of information with their appeal to these unconscious processes, takes full advantage of this knowledge.

All of us have experienced the inner fears, the uncertainties, the anxieties that seem to have been part of society as we know it. The internal dialogue, which says, "Oh my God, why did I do that?" or "What am I going to do?" or "Why don't I feel good?" ad infinitum may be part of the unconscious process that prevents us from dealing with the realities of existence. What if consciousness could assist in stopping this internal dialogue which often stands in the way of self-awareness? What better reason to try to find out what consciousness really is and what it means to us?

I believe that the explorations into consciousness can make a difference. The research must be continued and this new approach must be pursued.

Consider Carl Rogers' statement that "man is wiser than his intellect,"[18] and see if your consciousness tells you that this is true. And then consider the Islamic proverb:

> Three things cannot be retrieved:
> The arrow once sped from the bow
> The word spoken in haste
> The missed opportunity.[19]

2

ROBERT E. ORNSTEIN, PH.D.

A Science of Consciousness

A new synthesis and understanding are under way within the scientific community, and they are in part marked by this symposium. For the past several decades the study of mental phenomena in general, and consciousness in particular, has been underrepresented in psychology and related disciplines. It is often forgotten that "modern" psychology began as the science of conscious experience, of a meld of nineteenth-century science and philosophy.

The early psychologists and physiologists, such as Wundt, Fechner, and, later, William James and Titchener, found themselves challenged by the behaviorist doctrine of John Watson. Watson felt, quite reasonably, that the study of consciousness in psychology had led to a sterility in its content, and to controversies of only "academic" interest. The study of action, which was objective, verifiable, and quantifiable soon took over much, if not most, of psychology. New areas of concern such as the study of learning were opened up by the behaviorist "revolution" with, simultaneously, a parallel narrowing of range of interest. Problems were chosen which were amenable to solution only by behavioristic methods, and the original impetus to study psychology—the analysis of conscious experience—was soon lost.

Several recent developments have altered this picture. The most important is a sense in the academic community that we have left something out of our psychology of these past few years, something vital. We can no longer ignore the major cultural interest in "states of consciousness," alterations in mental states, the conceptual framework of the esoteric traditions. Indeed, it would be irresponsible to do so. Second, in the past decade, we have developed techniques which have enabled psychological researchers to go beyond the external "empty organism" view so popular in Watson's day and expounded today by his heirs such as Skinner. The study of dreams, for example, was put on a much more solid empirical basis by the advent of EEG-recording techniques for the monitoring of REM sleep in the 1950s. With the possibility of externally monitoring continuous brain states, many new areas of research opened up such as the psychophysiology of mental processes, and, more recently, biofeedback training. These share the possibility of developing an "external" correlate of internal physiological processes and its correlation with mental states. The introspectionist strategy of Titchener and his associates could be revived, and combined with methods of the technological age of psychology, in a new study of conscious experience.

In many areas of contemporary life this is a time, too, of synthesis and rapprochement. Within the scientific community the same currents flow, but more slowly, and more surely. Professor Lee has just considered many of these new ideas in such diverse areas as medicine, anthropology, physics, and philosophy, so there is little need here for repetition, except to say that the dominant paradigm in many of these disciplines is beginning to undergo a change, a shift away from the purely "rational, objective" emphasis of the first half of the twentieth century. This change does not indicate that the *basis* of science is in question, but that many areas of interest have not been given their full emphasis due to the dominance of methodological and technological advances in much of science. These trends have all too often obscured just those phenomena which were of the most interest. The study of consciousness is one of these areas of concern.

The synthesis in psychology, or the rapprochement, if you wish, combines the technological and methodological sophistication which we have so painstakingly developed in the past seventy-five years with conceptions drawn from philosophy and the ancient esoteric traditions. By this synthesis we do not indicate an armchair philosophical movement or a new attempt at metaphysical reductionism, but a realignment of the ideas of psychology and an extension of what we, as scientists, consider as possible for man. Research in the psychology of consciousness is the result of a true transplantation of a most specialized and sometimes hidden knowledge of human nature into the terms of the empirical tradition of the West. There is no attempt at preselling this knowledge (in the manner of the contemporary "growth center"), but we hope to subject some of the most important ideas about human nature to the conditions of our own scientific understanding. We will expect, then, that some of the more obscure and trivial ideas and claims of these sects will be found to be lacking in relevance and will drop out of consideration, while others, once restricted to an elite, may become the province of many within the culture. This is no question of one culture's or one tradition's superiority to another but of a differential specialization. As we in the West have specialized in an objective impersonal approach to knowledge, those in the East have specialized in a personal experiential approach. Both traditions have sought to transcend the limits of personal biases and distortions, one by a restriction to studies of external phenomena, the other by an attempt at the removal of the internal biases themselves. Neither methodology, however, is reducible to the other, nor are they necessarily antagonistic to one another, as has been previously thought.

To take an example, many of the seemingly abstruse and "esoteric" statements about man and the world can be considered within current understandings of brain function and of perception and cognition. Contemporary research has indicated that ordinary consciousness is an exquisitely evolved personal construction: sensory systems select a small amount of input data, the brain modifies and gates this sensory input, higher-level cortical selectivity filters on the basis of needs and preconceptions or "set." Although these ideas have recently caused a stir in academic circles with the "New Look" in perception,[1] the work of Adelbert Ames and his school,[2] and the work of Leon Festinger,[3] Karl Pribram,[4] and Roger Sperry,[5] these general ideas have been known to those of the esoteric traditions for centuries. The statement in esoteric and religious tradition, "The world is an illusion," is meant to convey this.

Here, too, is a good example of the nonreducibility of these statements. Roger Sperry's elegant theorizing on the role of the output systems of the brain and Leon Festinger's later experiments demonstrating the role of efferent processes in consciousness are hardly reducible to the statement "the world is an illusion." The psychologist's statements are about mechanism, about brain processes which subserve the internal awareness of occurrences. On the other side, the religious statement does not properly reduce to scientific descriptions of brain processes. "The world is an illusion" is intended as stimulus for personal investigation, in the context of one's life, and cannot be resolved merely by reading a description of a scientific experiment. The two areas do, however, have a common area of contact, which is the subject of this symposium, and of a science of consciousness.

Similarly, the idea of two modes of knowledge and the brain is the subject of much current interest, and, unfortunately, some misconstruction. "There are two modes of knowing, through argument and experience" wrote Roger

Bacon in the thirteenth century. Again, this has been at times considered "merely metaphysics," and has also been used to ignore the personal, intuitive component of knowledge. Many scientists have taken the word "experience" in its more restricted sense of *experiment* (indeed, in French they are the same word) and have ignored attempts to develop personal knowledge.

We now know that the two cerebral hemispheres of the human brain are divided in function. In most right-handed people the left hemisphere is predominantly involved in language and analytic mentation, while the right is predominantly involved in spatial mentation and operates in a manner described variously as synthetic or holistic.[6] I will make only a remark or two on these matters now for David Galin and I will present the results of our work in two papers later. I will say here that these specializations are not to be considered concretely as absolute entities, but as relative predominances of one hemisphere or another.

One should not, for instance, decide that he or she "completely understands" the practices of esoteric traditions simply because it is useful to conceive of them as specializations of the right hemisphere. To take the counter example: one might realize intellectually that "language predominantly depends upon the left hemisphere of the brain," but this does not constitute *learning language*. We should recognize, however, that we are biologically equipped to process information in two distinct and complementary modes which are developed in different manners.

But once we consider that our capabilities for knowledge are, perhaps, greater than had been previously thought within the scientific community, we must also beware of the extravagant claims and the misuse of science for commercial ends. If we can credit that the sometimes bizarre and seemingly disconnected meditation exercises may have a common basis, it does not automatically mean that everyone should take up meditation. In several instances, "Science" has been used to further a commercial endeavor, e.g., some research on meditation, which has attempted to "sell" the technique on the basis that it can produce physiological changes. Whether these "changes" are to be considered desirable, or are unique to a given technique, is never mentioned in the barrage of undigested data which is presented. This is simply a perversion of science and a cheapening of the esoteric traditions— there is an almost comic synthesis here of the spiritual advancement of the West and the technological sophistication of the East. Because so many early and extravagant mistakes are committed means neither that the study of consciousness is entirely worthless nor that electric or transcendental bliss is around the corner.

Additional difficulties extend to the area of biofeedback training, which is a synthesis of Eastern ideas of extended self-regulation and contemporary electrophysiological methods developed in the past fifteen years. These techniques hold great promise for many, in the self-control of muscle activity, of heart, and possibly of brain activity. But, as with the over-sell of meditation, biofeedback has become a stimulus for the popular imagination without being scientifically grounded. In the eyes of many it was fad passed over in 1973. The commercial market is currently glutted with $79.95 alpha machines which promise eternal bliss (and many other things). None of the currently available commercial equipment are useful to the ordinary person, in spite of their promise, since this technology has not been fully developed.

I could continue to document many other bizarre and sometimes naïve errors in attempts to study consciousness scientifically, but to no real point. We would hope in this symposium and in later work to open a new *kind* of investigation in this area: an investigation by scientists, newly interested in many of the questions which have intrigued many in philosophy and theology over the centuries, an investigation performed for the first time within the mainstream of contemporary science. A science of consciousness itself presupposes such a confluence; many of the most important aspects of man's questioning of himself, his nature, the nature of the world will finally get their "day in court," free from the prejudices which have kept them out for so long, and free of the biased claims of the fanatics and the armchair metaphysicians.

It is our hope in this symposium to consider a very few elements of this new science: research on the two sides of the brain, implications of our biological duality, research on meditation and differing modes of appreciation of reality, and a proposal for a new strategy for research in consciousness involving the concept of "discrete states" of consciousness.

3

DAVID GALIN, M. D.

The Two Modes of Consciousness and the Two Halves of the Brain

The Ants and the Pen
(a fourteenth-century tale from the Middle East).

An ant one day strayed across a piece of paper and saw a pen writing in fine, black strokes.

"How wonderful this is," said the ant. "This remarkable thing, with a life of its own, makes squiggles on this beautiful surface, to such an extent and with such energy that it is equal to the efforts of all the ants in the world. And the squiggles which it makes! These resemble ants: not one, but millions, all run together."

He repeated his ideas to another ant, who was equally interested. He praised the powers of observation and reflection of the first ant.

But another ant said: "Profiting, it must be admitted, by your efforts, I have observed this strange object. But I have determined that it is not the master of this work. You failed to notice that this pen is attached to certain other objects, which surround it and drive it on its way. These should be considered as the moving factor, and given credit." Thus were fingers discovered by the ants.

But another ant, after a long time, climbed over the fingers and realised that they comprised a hand, which he thoroughly explored, after the manner of ants, by scrambling all over it.

He returned to his fellows: "Ants," he cried, "I have news of importance for you. Those smaller objects are a part of a large one. It is this which gives motion to them."

But then it was discovered that the hand was attached to an arm, and the arm to a body, and that there were two hands, and that there were feet which did no writing.

The investigations continue. Of the mechanics of the writing, the ants have a fair idea. Of the meaning and intention of the writing, and how it is ultimately controlled, they will not find out by their customary method of investigation. Because they are "literate."[1]

Light the Candle

Nasrudin was sitting talking with a friend as dusk fell. "Light a candle," the man said, "because it is dark now. There is one just by your left side." "How can I tell my right from my left in the dark, you fool?" asked the Mulla.[2]

As these ancient stories illustrate, there is more than one way of knowledge, more than one way of validating experience. In addition to the linear, logical approach which proceeds piecemeal, step by step, as in the "ants' science," there is another mode which is intuitive and holistic, which grasps the relations between the parts directly rather than by a sequence of deductions.

These two aspects of our nature, sometimes complementary, sometimes in conflict, have been pointed out in art, philosophy, religion, and literature for thousands of years; a contemporary example is Polanyi's exposition of "tacit and explicit knowledge."[3]

For the past five years Robert Ornstein and I have been exploring brain mechanisms relating to consciousness. We believe that these two ways of knowing are related to the specialization of the two cerebral hemispheres for different cognitive modes. The study of how these two half-brains co-operate or interfere with each other has just begun. We believe that this work has important implications beyond experimental neuropsychology; it has lead us into major issues in education, psychiatry, anthropology, and philosophy.

HEMISPHERIC SPECIALIZATION

It has been known for one hundred years that in typical right handers the left hemisphere is specialized for spoken language and its derivatives, reading and writing. A large injury to the left hemisphere will usually destroy these behaviors. An injury to the right hemisphere does not usually interfere with speech, and for a long time the right hemisphere was considered to be just a rather stupid spare for the left. The specialization of the right hemisphere has only recently been widely recognized; it is very good at dealing with novel complex spatial and musical patterns. A person with a large right-hemisphere injury might have trouble copying a geometric figure, or matching a design with wooden blocks, or recognizing faces (even his own), or recognizing melodies. These tasks all require that you keep in mind an *over-all pattern of relations*, not just the separate parts.

It is important to emphasize that what most characterizes the hemispheres is not that they are specialized to work with different types of material (the left with words and the right with spatial forms); rather, each hemisphere is specialized for a different cognitive style; the left for an analytic, logical mode for which words are an excellent tool, and the right for a holistic, Gestalt mode, which happens to be particularly suitable for spatial relations.

THE TWO COGNITIVE MODES CHARACTERIZED

We have called the style of the left hemisphere "analytical"; i.e., it is adept at taking things apart, and dealing with the separated parts one at a time. In this mode, therefore, boundaries are very important, because boundaries are what define a part.

Words serve to establish boundaries. When we name an object (or a person) we separate it from its context, and label it in accord with some of its attributes, of necessity neglecting other attributes. For example, if I say "give me the hammer," I have focused attention on the functional aspects of the tool (hammer, rather than the pliers) and not on its size, color, ownership, sentimental or cash value, etc. In this sense labeling is a way of excluding aspects or relations which are not wanted. This is why people often resent being " labeled"; the label of necessity excludes some aspect, and they do not want any aspect of themselves to be denied. This is exemplified currently in the feminists' concern over labels pertaining to gender.

Sequence or temporal ordering is also very important in the analytic mode. In verbal analysis, for example, word sequence is critical to meaning in sentences (compare "John loves Mary" versus "Mary loves John"). Injuries to the left hemisphere interfere with the perception of temporal sequences. Patients with such injuries may not be able to tell which of two lights flashed first, or if they flashed at the same time. We have speculated that this specialization for temporal ordering in simple perceptual and motor performance may be related to a focus on time in more complex behavior. For example, this mode might emphasize concern with outcome and sequences of actions, focusing on the future, or the past, rather than focusing on processes and the present (what Gestalt therapists call "staying in the now").

The verbal-analytic style is extremely efficient for dealing with the object world. Our modern technology, standard of living, and scientific achievements depend heavily on highly developed linear, analytic methods. Communication of some concepts is very difficult without verbal propositions; for example, "Democracy requires informed participation." On the other hand, some concepts are not handled well with words. Consider what most people do when asked to define a spiral staircase: they begin to say a few words haltingly, and then make a twirling gesture with an upraised finger. For most people this complex concept is better handled with this visual-kinesthetic representation than with a verbal representation. (One of our associates whose earlier training was in nuclear physics answered with the sine and cosine equations for a helix, without moving his hands, but this is not a common response.) This sort of nonverbal representation seems to be more characteristic of right-hemisphere thinking.

We have called the special style of the right hemisphere "holistic." It is particularly good at grasping patterns of relations. This mode seems to integrate many inputs simultaneously, rather than operating on them one at a time, sequentially, like the analytic mode. This is important for the many situations in which the essential meaning is given by the overall pattern of relations between the elements, not by the elements themselves. A simple example of this is a stew; its nature depends on the mutual interactions of its parts. A piece of meat, a potato, a carrot, an onion, a clove of garlic, cooked and served separately in sequence would not be stew; they must simultaneously act on each other.

The holistic mode of information processing is very good for bridging gaps; we can perceive a pattern even when some of the pieces are missing. In contrast, a logical, sequential mode cannot skip over gaps. Since we are usually trying to operate in this world with incomplete information, we very badly need to have a capacity to perceive general patterns and jump across gaps in present knowledge.

HEMISPHERIC DISCONNECTION SYNDROME—"THE SPLIT BRAIN"

The two hemispheres have been surgically separated for the treatment of certain rare cases of epilepsy. It has been found that after all the connecting nerve-fiber bundles have been cut, each hemisphere is independently conscious and can carry out the complex cognitive processes of the type for which it is specialized. In short, there appear to be two separate, conscious minds in one head. Sperry has summarized the hemispheric disconnection syndrome as follows:

The most remarkable effect of sectioning the cerebral commissures continues to be the apparent lack of change with respect to ordinary behavior. [The patients] . . . exhibit no gross alterations of personality, intellect or overt behavior two years after operation. Individual mannerisms, conversation and bearing, temperament, strength, vigor and coordination are all largely intact and seem much as before surgery. Despite this outward appearance of general normality in ordinary behavior . . . specific tests indicate functional disengagement of the right and left hemispheres with respect to nearly all cognitive and other psychic activities. Learning and memory are found to proceed quite independently in each separated hemisphere. Each hemisphere seems to have its own conscious sphere for sensation, perception, ideation, and other mental activities and the whole inner realm of gnostic experience of the one is cut off from the corresponding experiences of the other hemisphere —with only a few exceptions . . . .[4]

To understand the method of testing and interviewing each half of the brain separately, two points of functional anatomy must be kept in mind. The first is that since language functions (speech, writing) are mediated predominantly by the left hemisphere in most people, the disconnected right hemisphere cannot express itself verbally. The second point is that the neural pathways carrying information from one side of the body and one-half of the visual field cross over and connect only with the opposite side of the brain. This means that sensations in the right hand and images in the right visual space will be projected almost entirely to the *left* hemisphere. Similarly, the major motor output is crossed, and the left hemisphere controls mainly the movements of the right hand. Therefore, patients with the two hemispheres disconnected can describe or answer questions about objects placed in their right hands, or pictures flashed to the right visual fields with a tachistoscope, but can give no correct verbal response when the information is presented to the left hand or the left visual field (they will, in fact, often confabulate). However, the mute right hemisphere can indicate its experience with the left hand, for example, by selecting the proper object from an array.

Figure 1 shows a view of the human brain, from the top, looking down on the cerebral hemispheres. It is something like a walnut from this view, wrinkly and divided down the middle into two distinct halves by a deep fissure. At the bottom of the fissure (not seen in this figure) the two halves are connected by a great bridge of nerve fibers called the Corpus Callosum. From a side view the brain is more like a mushroom, with the hemispheres forming the cap, and the lower parts of the brain forming a stem which connects below with the spinal cord. Figure 2 shows a side view in which the brain has been sliced into two halves by cutting along the fissure through the Corpus Callosum, and down through the stem; the figure shows the cut (medial) surface. Figure 3 is another view from above, in which the top of the cerebrum has been sliced off or dissected away, in order to show some of the fibers of the Corpus Callosum sweeping across the fissure and connecting matching points in the two hemispheres. This dissection gives a good view of how extensive a structure the Corpus Callosum is: it contains 200,000,000 nerve fibers, more than the combined total of all the sensory fibers entering the cerebrum and all the descending fibers controlling movement. From its relative size, it would appear to be a very important part of the brain. Nevertheless, when this connecting bridge was surgically cut, the patients seemed quite ordinary unless tested in the very special ways described above.

DISSOCIATION OF EXPERIENCE

The dissociation between the experiences of the two disconnected hemispheres is sometimes very dramatic. Dr. Roger Sperry and his colleagues at the California Institute of Technology have photographed illustrative incidents. One film study shows a female patient being tested with a tachistoscope as described above. In the series of neutral geometrical figures being presented at random to the right and left fields, a nude pin-up was included and flashed to the right (nonverbal) hemisphere. The patient blushes and giggles. Sperry asks "What did you see?" She answers "Nothing, just a flash of light," and giggles again, covering her mouth

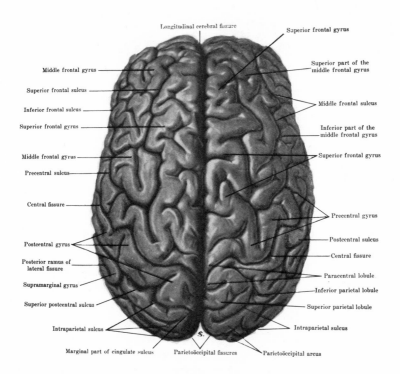

FIGURE 1.
From F. Mettler, *Neuroanatomy*. St. Louis: Mosby Co., 1948, p. 83.

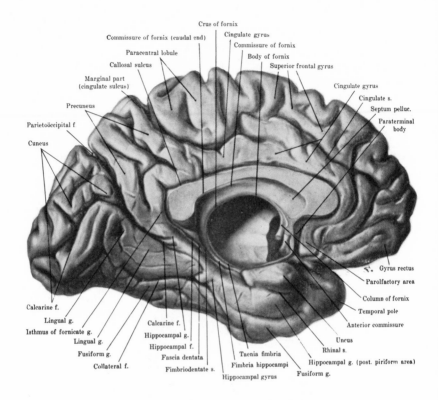

FIGURE 2.

From F. Mettler, *Neuroanatomy*. St. Louis: Mosby Co., p. 99.

with her hand. "Why are you laughing then?" asks Sperry, and she laughs again and says, "Oh, Dr. Sperry, you have some machine." The episode is very suggestive; if one did not know her neurosurgical history one might see this as a clear example of perceptual defense and think that she was "repressing" the perception of the disturbing sexual material— even her final response (a socially acceptable non sequitur) was convincing.

In another film a different patient is performing a block-design task; he is trying to match a colored geometric design with a set of painted blocks. The film shows the left hand (right hemisphere) quickly carrying out the task. Then the experimenter disarranges the blocks and the right hand (left hemisphere) is given the task; slowly and with great apparent indecision it arranges the pieces. In trying to match a corner of the design the right hand corrects one of the blocks, and then shifts it again, apparently not realizing it was correct; the viewer sees the left hand dart out, grab the block to restore it to the correct position—and then the arm of the experimenter reaches over and pulls the intruding left hand off camera.

FIGURE 3.

From *Cunningham's Textbook of Anatomy.* Ed. J. C. Brash. New York: Oxford University Press, 1951. 9th edition, p. 962.

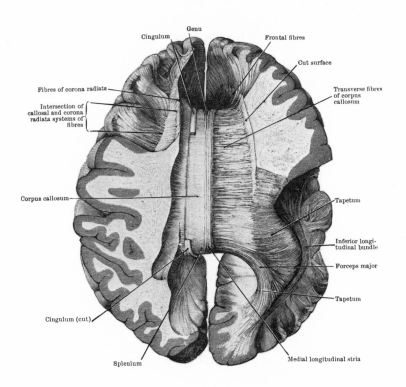

Dr. Joseph Bogen, one of the surgeons who performed the split-brain operations, has published some results from drawing tests which he conducted with his patients after the operation.[5] These tests illustrate in a simple way the basic difference between the two hemispheres in their capacities for holistic processes.

Figure 4 shows two geometric designs, a cross and a cube, which Bogen asked the patients to copy, and samples of their productions with the right and left hands. The copies with the left hand (controlled by the right hemisphere) are fairly good representations of the model; although the draughtsmanship is crude, the essence of the form is preserved. The patient was very reluctant to try the task with his right hand (controlled by the left hemisphere), protesting that it was too difficult, that he was never good at drawing, etc., although he had just done the left-hand copies without hesitation. The right hand's copy of the cross preserves the *elements* of the form (a sequence of connected right angles), but the essence of the form, the configuration or Gestalt, is lost. The attempt to copy the cube with the right hand shows the same phenomenon; the most basic elements, the lines, are given without the articulation which constitutes the form. Figure 5 shows similar examples from another patient.

In contrast to the successful left-handed performances on the drawing tests, these patients were unable to write even the date or the day of the week from dictation with their left hands; and although their right hands could not copy forms they could easily write spontaneously or to dictation. This lateral dissociation between copying and writing showed very little recovery in those patients who had a normal childhood neurological development. It was less persistent in those whose brain injuries dated from birth or early childhood, presumably because early injury leads to compensation by other brain structures, and less lateral specialization.

Figure 6 shows characteristic disability in the writing and

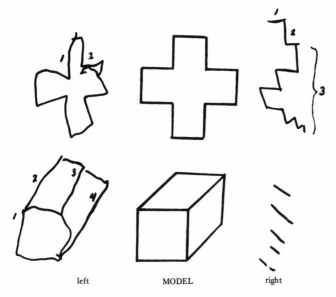

left	MODEL	right

FIGURE 4.

Both figures from J. E. Bogen, "The Other Side of the Brain I: Dysgraphia and Dyscopia following Commissurotomy," *Bulletin of the Los Angeles Neurological Society*, 1969.

FIGURE 5.

drawing of a patient five years after commissurotomy. Dr. Bogen observed:

> With his left hand he drew what looks as if it might be a "P" and then stopped and shook his head. He was asked what this was and said "I was trying to write my name [Bill]." He was then asked to write something with his right hand and he wrote the sentence in the upper right hand corner. He was then asked to attempt again with his left hand and produced only the small scrawl which is seen in the upper left hand corner. He was then shown a model of the Greek cross; he copied it with his left hand. The arrow which was added later indicates that he started at the top of the figure and drew the entire figure with a single continuous line. He was then asked to copy the same model with his right hand; he drew the strokes in the order indicated. He finished only the first six

FIGURE 6.
From Bogen, "The Other Side of the Brain I."

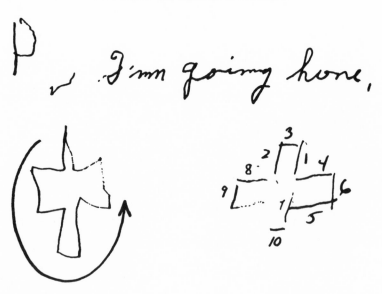

strokes; he was then urged to continue and he added the seventh. When persuaded to add some more, he put in the concluding three strokes and then stopped. When asked if he was done, he said, "Yes."[6]

Bogen's description highlights the difference in the processes by which the two hands copy the Greek cross. The left hand executes the figure in a smooth continuous motion; it forms a Gestalt. The right hand, which had shown some improvement in the five years since surgery, proceeded part by part, as indicated by the sequence of the strokes.

HOW DO THE TWO HEMISPHERES GET ALONG UNDER NORMAL CIRCUMSTANCES?

Two facts have been presented: the cerebral hemispheres are specialized for different kinds of thinking, and when they are surgically disconnected, each one is capable of being independently conscious. When these two facts are considered together they lead to a number of important questions. In the normal person with intact connections between the hemispheres, are these systems smoothly integrated? Can these two half-brains to some extent sustain separate parallel consciousnesses as they do when the connecting fibers are surgically severed? Or do they alternate in control, taking turns in directing behavior? If they can operate independently, there are possibilities for both cooperation and for conflict. Bogen has pointed out some of the implications of these two facts, summarizing the main propositions very elegantly and with proper historical perspective, under the title of "Neowiganism."

The essentials of this theory and its implications were first developed by A. L. Wigan in a book called *The Duality of the Mind* published in 1844. Wigan was first led to his theory by the postmortem observation of a man whom he had known well before the man's death from unrelated causes. At autopsy one cerebral hemisphere was found to be totally absent. Wigan was not only astounded by this finding, but had the wits to see its meaning: only one hemisphere is required to have a mind or to be a person. Therefore Wigan concluded: if only one cerebrum is required to have a mind, possession of two hemispheres (the normal state) makes possible or perhaps even inevitable the possession of two minds; and however synchronous these two minds may be most of the time, there must inevitably be some occasion when they are discrepant. This provides the anatomical-physiologic basis for that division of self, that internal struggle which is characteristic of so much of mankind's ill health and unhappiness. This magnificent speculation was accorded very little notice at the time. . . . What Wigan did not know [was that] . . . whereas the two hemispheres of a cat or monkey may sustain two duplicate minds, the lateralization typical of man requires that the two minds must *necessarily* be discrepant. "Neowiganism" means that . . . each of us is possessed of two minds which differ in content, possibly even goals, but most certainly in respect to mode of organization. The evolutionary advantage of having two different minds is obvious; possession of two independent problem solving organs increases mightily the likelihood of a creative solution to a novel problem. At the same time there is an enormous increase in the likelihood of internal conflict. And so we have man, the most innovative of species and at the same time the most at odds with himself.[7]

LEFT AND RIGHT MODES:
COMPLEMENTARY OR IN CONFLICT

The analytic and holistic modes are complementary; each provides a dimension which the other lacks. Artists, scientists, mathematicians, writing about their own creativity, all report that their work is based on a smooth integration of both modes. If we want to cultivate creativity it appears that we must first develop each mode, both the rational-analytic and the intuitive-holistic; second, we must develop the ability to inhibit either one when it is inappropriate to the task at hand; and finally we must be able to operate in both modes in a complementary fashion.

However, the two modes may also be in conflict; there seems to be some mutual antagonism between the analytic and the holistic. For example, the tendency of the left hemisphere to note details in a form suitable for expression in words seems to interfere with the perception of the over-all pattern. This mutual interference has been suggested as the reason why our brains evolved with these two systems segregated into separate hemispheres.

Use of the inappropriate mode for a task may account for some common problems. My difficulties with dancing may be related to my excessive reliance on analytic sequential processes; instead of allowing a smooth synthesis of the separate parts, I have not been able to progress past counting "one . . . two . . . THREE . . . , one . . . two . . . THREE." Similarly, an excessive or inappropriate use of the holistic mode could interfere with learning to read, or with carrying out sequential arithmetic calculations such as are required in balancing a checkbook.

The specialization of the hemispheres and their potential for independent functioning may play some role in psychiatric conflict as well.[8] Freud had reluctantly abandoned the attempt to relate the functioning of the parts of the mental apparatus to specific anatomical locations because the neurology of his time was insufficient. It may be useful to reconsider these questions now.

There is a compelling formal similarity between some dissociations seen in the split-brain patients (such as the pin-up sequence described above) and the phenomena of repression. According to Freud's early "topographical" model of the mind, repressed mental contents functioned in a separate realm which was inaccessible to conscious recall or verbal interrogation. This realm of the unconscious had its own rules, and developed its own goals. It could affect the viscera, and could insinuate itself into the stream of ongoing consciously directed behavior. Certain aspects of right-hemisphere functioning are similar to "primary process," the form of thought which Freud originally assigned to the unconscious realm: both depend mainly on nonverbal image representations, with nonsyllogistic logic, and are more concerned with multiple simultaneous interactions than with temporal sequencing.

When the two hemispheres are surgically disconnected the mental process of each one is inaccessible to deliberate conscious retrieval from the point of view of the other. However, the operation does not affect them as symmetrically with respect to overt behavior. Sperry and his collaborators have found that "in general, the postoperative behavior [of the patients] has been dominated by the major [left] hemisphere . . ." except in tasks for which the right hemisphere is particularly specialized.[9] In these respects there seems to be a parallel between the functioning of the isolated right hemisphere and mental processes which are repressed, unconscious, and unable directly to control behavior.

These similarities suggest the hypothesis that in normal, intact people mental events in the right hemisphere can become disconnected functionally from the left hemisphere (by inhibition of neuronal transmission across the Corpus Callosum) and can continue a life of their own. This hypothesis offers a neurophysiological mechanism for at least some instances of repression, and an anatomical locus for the unconscious mental contents.

HOW INTEGRATED ARE THE TWO HEMISPHERES
UNDER NORMAL CONDITIONS?

We do not know the usual relation between the two hemispheres in normal adults, but we can speculate on several possible arrangements. One possibility is that they operate in alternation. i.e., taking turns, depending on situational demands. When one hemisphere is "on" it may inhibit the other. A variant of this relationship might be that the dominating hemisphere makes use of one or more of the subsystems of the other hemisphere (e.g., memory), inhibiting the rest (e.g., planning, motivation). The inhibition thus may be only partial, suppressing enough of the subordinate hemisphere so as to render it incapable of sustaining its own plan of action. Our EEG studies of normal people are consistent with this view: when subjects performed verbal tasks (left hemisphere) we observed an increase in alpha waves (an idling rhythm) over the right hemisphere; when they performed spatial tasks (right hemisphere) the idling rhythm shifted to the left hemisphere.[10] Another variant is the one hypothesized above in relation to "repression"; one hemisphere dominates overt behavior, but can only disconnect rather than totally inhibit (disrupt) the other hemisphere, which remains independently conscious. The fourth possible condition, in which the two hemispheres are fully active and integrated with each other, is the condition which Bogen associates with creativity.[11] Unfortunately this does not seem to occur very often. In fact, he suggests that one of the reasons that the commissurotomy patients appear so normal to casual observation is because the activities of daily life do not demand much creativity.

If the usual condition is either alternation between the two modes, or parallel but independent consciousnesses with one of them dominating overt behavior, what factors determine which hemisphere will be "on"? Which will gain control of the shared functions and dominate overt behavior? There are two factors suggested by experiments with split-brain monkeys and humans. One could be called "resolution by speed"; the hemisphere which solves the problem first gets to the output channel first. This seems the most likely explanation for the observations in the human patients that "when a hemisphere is intrinsically better equipped to handle some task, it is also easier for that hemisphere to dominate the motor pathways."[9]

For example, Sperry and his collaborators have found that the right hemisphere dominates behavior in a facial recognition task. Recognition of faces requires a perception of the Gestalt, and is relatively resistant to analytical verbal description.

A second factor determining which hemisphere gets control could be called "resolution by motivation"; the one who cares more about the outcome pre-empts the output. This was demonstrated by Michael Gazzaniga in a series of ingenious experiments with split-brain monkeys. He taught each hemisphere (separately) the opposite solutions to a discrimination task, and then tested them at the same time, in conflict. He found that he could change which hemisphere dominated behavior by changing the amount of reward that each hemisphere got for a correct answer. Gazzaniga concluded "Cerebral dominance in monkeys is quite flexible and subject to the effects of reinforcement. . . . The hemisphere which is most successful in earning reinforcement comes to dominate."[12] This may apply to intact humans as well. As the left hemisphere develops its language capability in the second and third year of life it gains a great advantage over the right hemisphere in manipulating its environment and securing reinforcements. It seems likely to me that this is the basis for the left hemisphere's suzerainty in overt behavior in situations of conflict with the right hemisphere.

CONDITIONS FAVORING THE DEVELOPMENT
OF SEPARATE STREAMS OF CONSCIOUSNESS

There are several ways in which the two hemispheres of an ordinary person could begin to function as if they had been surgically disconnected and decrease their exchange of information.

The first way is by active inhibition of information transfer because of conflict. Imagine the effect on a child when his mother presents one message verbally but quite another with her facial expression and body language; "I am doing it because I love you, dear," say the words, but "I hate you and will destroy you," says the face. Each hemisphere is exposed to the same sensory input, but because of their relative specializations, they each emphasize only one of the messages. The left will attend to the verbal cues because it cannot extract information from the facial Gestalt efficiently; the right will attend to the nonverbal cues because it cannot easily understand the words. In effect, a different input has been delivered to each hemisphere, just as in the laboratory experiments in which a tachistoscope is used to present different pictures to the left and right visual fields. I offer the following conjecture: in this situation the two hemispheres might decide on opposite courses of action; the left to approach, and the right to flee. Because of the high stakes involved each hemisphere might be able to maintain its consciousness and resist the inhibitory influence of the other side. The left hemisphere seems to win control of the output channels most of the time, but if the left is not able to "turn off" the right completely it may settle for disconnecting the transfer of the conflicting information from the other side. The connections between hemispheres are relatively weak compared to the connections within hemispheres, and it seems likely that each hemisphere treats the weak contralateral input in the same way in which people in general treat the odd discrepant observation which does not fit with the mass of their beliefs; first they ignore it, and then, if it is insistent, they actively avoid it.

The mental process in the right hemisphere, cut off in this way from the left-hemisphere consciousness which is directing overt behavior, may nevertheless continue a life of its own. The memory of the situation, the emotional concomitants, and the frustrated plan of action all may persist, affecting subsequent perception and forming the basis for expectations and evaluations of future input.

DICHOTOMANIA

The notion that there is a relation between the duality of the human brain and other dualities in human nature has been taken up by people in many different fields besides neuropsychology: for example, in education, sociology, the creative arts, philosophy. Like many productive ideas, this one is sometimes applied overenthusiastically. The specialization of the two halves of the brain is being offered as the mechanism underlying everybody's favorite pair of polar opposites: scientist-artist, obsessive-hysteric, rational-mystical, conscious-unconscious, masculine-feminine. Marcel Kinsbourne has labeled this phenomenon in its excesses "dichotomania."

The problem is a new version of "naïve localizationism," which grew up with the phrenologists of the eighteenth century. The phrenologists made an important contribution to neuropsychology in advancing the idea that the different parts of the brain were not functionally identical This idea was expanded, however, into the thesis that if certain capacities were more developed in an individual the corresponding part of the brain would be larger, and this would be detectable in a corresponding bump on the skull. They produced detailed maps, such as Figure 7, localizing complex psychological qualities to minute areas of the scalp. (Note the close association between combativeness and conjugality.)

Naïve localizationism is not just an antique curiosity. As recently as the 1930s a distinguished neurologist (Kleist) was publishing maps like that shown in Figure 8, with a mosaic of functional labels superimposed on a drawing of the convolutions of the cerebrum. This sort of thinking is perpetuated today when complex behaviors or capacities are treated as if they were unitary, to be carried out by discrete areas or subsystems of the brain; e.g., "the left hemisphere does arithmetic," or in the extreme form, "the left angular gyrus. . . ." This arises in part from observations that certain behavioral

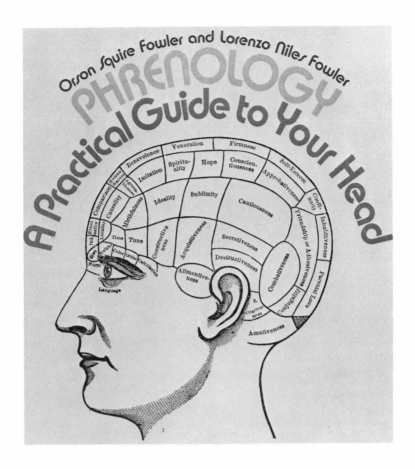

FIGURE 7.

deficits tend to follow injury to certain brain areas. Macdonald Critchley notes, "there are certain vulnerable regions of the brain wherein a lesion is more apt to be followed by a severe dyscalculia bearing certain clinical hallmarks. Thus disease of the dominant left hemisphere is more often followed by severe disorders of calculation."[13] But Critchley is careful to point out that arithmetic may entail more than one type of mentation and that different people seem to employ

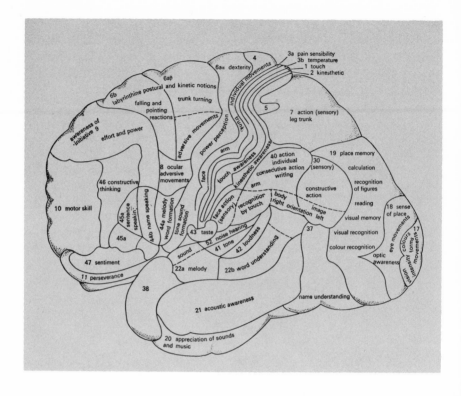

FIGURE 8.

different methods. To a certain extent, arithmetic does require analytic sequential processes; we follow an algorithm in step-by-step fashion, not skipping around or leaving anything out. On the other hand, the horizontal and vertical arrangement of numbers to represent units, tens, hundreds, etc., depends on spatial and constructional factors. Vivid imagery for numerical forms and sequences may be important to some people. Therefore Critchley concludes that lesions in several different areas can be expected to interfere with arithmetic insofar as a person depends on the use of specific visual symbols or notation, or on rote memory (e.g., multiplication tables), or on an ideokinetic factor based on concrete manipulation such as counting on fingers.

It should be noted that higher mathematics is very different from arithmetic, and is much more likely to involve some component of multidimensional spatial representations. Most great mathematicians have written about the importance of intuition in mathematics, stressing that linear reasoning is not enough. Einstein described his own mathematical thinking as follows: "The physical entities which seem to serve as elements in thought are certain signs and more or less clear images . . . [in] combinatory play. . . . The above-mentioned elements are, in my case, of visual and some of muscular type. Conventional words or other signs have to be sought for laboriously only in a secondary stage, when the above-mentioned associative play is sufficiently established and can be reproduced at will. . . ."

An illustration of how this sort of localizationism can distort the concept of lateral cerebral specialization is shown in the comparison of Figures 9 and 10.

Figure 9 is the cover from Robert Ornstein's psychology textbook. The painting was intended as a metaphorical or shorthand statement for some of the ideas and speculations elaborated and qualified in the text. The mathematician, the lawyer, the scientist are shown on the left, representing not specific skills, but rather a style of information processing, in this case verbal, analytical, and sequential. On the right are the craftsman, the sculptor, the dancer, representing processes depending on holistic thought, the integration of multiple simultaneous inputs, or the consideration of patterns in which the Gestalt is more important than the sequence of the parts. Notice also several mandalas which are used as tools for meditation in certain disciplines. A sleeper is shown with his head in a cloudy dream about a magic city. On both sides, we see Nasrudin, a famous wiseman-fool character from Middle Eastern folklore, who figures prominently in Sufi teaching materials. He appears on both sides and in the middle, like the Corpus Callosum, trying to bring the two hemispheres (two ways of knowing) into communication with each other;

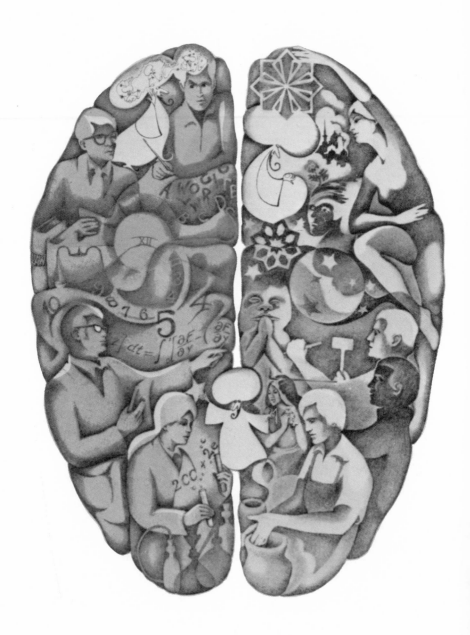

FIGURE 9.

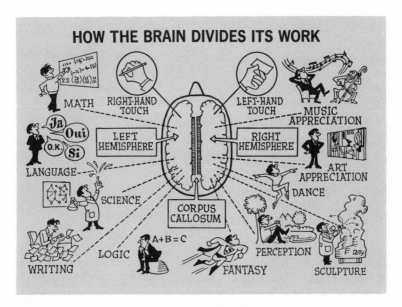

FIGURE 10.
Roy Doty

he wanders freely, at home on either side, and bridging the gap.

Figure 10 shows a version of this metaphor taken literally, schematized for an article in the science column of *Newsweek* magazine. Nasrudin is gone, and the metaphor is concretized to the level of a wiring diagram; e.g., "the left hemisphere does arithmetic."

A much prettier and more sophisticated graphic metaphor for the proposed lateral duality appeared on the cover of *The New York Times Magazine* (Figure 11). The photographer Peter Simon restricted himself to portraying a single sort of behavior, the dance. He emphasized that what is different about the two hemispheres is the way they treat the same subject; it is more a difference of style than content. The left hemisphere views dance as does a dictionary definition; the emphasis is on logical precision and exhaustive categoriza-

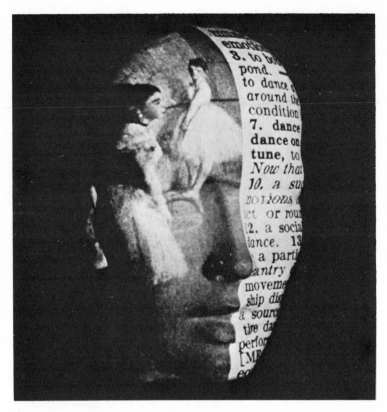

FIGURE 11.
Photo by Peter Angelo Simon.

tion. The right-hemisphere treatment is more open-ended, expressed in forms and images whose boundaries are rather fuzzy, a set of suggestions as to what dance is about without specifying all the details. This illustration captures the concept that dance, or the knowledge of dance, is not assigned to just one hemisphere; both have their competences, vis-à-vis dance, in their own special ways. This treatment is much more resistant to a naïve, concrete localizationism or to a simple-minded dichotomania. We can avoid slipping into a neophrenology by keeping in mind that we are talking about styles of information processing, not specific contents.

4

ROBERT E. ORNSTEIN, PH.D., AND DAVID GALIN, M. D.

Physiological Studies of Consciousness

One major approach to the study of human consciousness is through an analysis of corresponding brain mechanisms. Although the scientific study of subjective experience per se has a long and productive history in psychology,* the correlative study of brain and consciousness provides several unique advantages.

First, consideration of neural structure can provide guidance in psychological theory construction. Neuroanatomical divisions in the brain may, for instance, provide clues to divisions and relationships in cognition and subjective experience. Second, in experiments in which consciousness and ongoing physiological processes can be studied simultaneously, an external indicator of private experience can be developed. The internal experience can never be reduced to its external indicators, but such indicators may prove quite useful simply in marking the occurrence of a certain experience, as rapid eye movements and low-voltage fast EEG during sleep mark the occurrence of dreaming.

* For a recent example, see the essay by Tart in this volume.

In our laboratory at the University of California Medical Center, we have been studying a relationship of brain activity to consciousness, employing EEG and other objective measures to chart subjective experience. As described in the previous chapter, there is a wide variety of clinical and neurosurgical evidence to indicate that the human brain is laterally specialized for different cognitive modes. (The left hemisphere tends to operate in a sequential manner suitable for language and analysis of information, the right hemisphere tends to a simultaneous mode suitable for organization of spatial thought and for synthesis of information.) These modes can complement each other but cannot readily substitute for each other. Employing the inappropriate cognitive system may not only be inefficient, it may actually interfere with processing in the appropriate system. Jerre Levy has in fact suggested that the human brain has evolved with verbal and nonverbal functions in separate hemispheres to reduce the interference of one system with the other.[1] This "interference hypothesis" is supported by her study of left-handed subjects who often have language representation in both hemispheres. She compared left- and right-handed subjects with equal verbal IQ scores, and found that left handers had significantly lower spatial scores, which she attributed to interference from the presumed ambilaterality of language. Similarly, in a group of neurosurgical patients in whom right-hemisphere language was demonstrated, the more that language was established in the right hemisphere, the worse was the spatial performance.[2]

We have attempted to extend the study of the two modes of consciousness and the human brain beyond the effects of pathology and neurosurgery. We are primarily concerned with the implications of this evidence for the study of normal people. Do normal people doing ordinary, everyday things make use of the lateral specialization of the brain? And, if so, what is the nature of such specialization in ordinary people?

If the two modes interfere with one another, then by recording the EEG from both hemispheres of a normal person working at a cognitive task we might be able to see a sign of the selective activation and suppression of these two hemispheres.

We tried out these ideas on a trusty medical student assigned to us for the summer. We outfitted him with EEG electrodes over the left and right temporal and parietal areas, asked him to perform verbal and spatial tasks—to write a letter and to arrange a set of colored blocks to match a given pattern. While writing (a presumably left-hemisphere task) he produced a high-amplitude EEG over the right hemisphere and much less amplitude over the left hemisphere. The high amplitude seemed to be contributed mainly by the alpha rhythm (waves at approximately 10 cycles per second). This pattern reversed while he was arranging blocks, with the alpha dominant over the left hemisphere and less visible over the right hemisphere. The alpha rhythm is generally taken to indicate a diminution of information-processing (colloquially a "turning off") in the area involved. This seemed to be what we were searching for, a measure of selective activation and suppression of the two hemispheres in a normal person. The left hemisphere "idled" while our student was arranging the blocks; the right hemisphere idled while he was writing. We retested him all summer and tested other laboratory personnel as well and found similar results: their EEGs showed (for each cognitive mode) that the area of the brain *not* being used was relatively "turned off."

Figures 1A and 1B illustrate the EEGs recorded from normal subjects while engaged in these cognitive activities. Note the appearance of the high-amplitude alpha in the left hemisphere (EEG lead T_3) during the presentation of spatial problem situations, and the greater alpha in the right hemisphere (T_4) during work on verbal and arithmetic tasks.

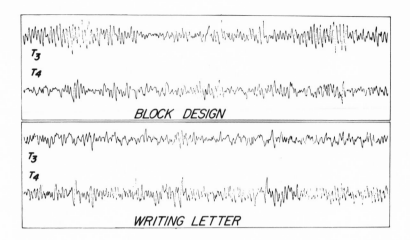

FIGURE 1A.

With these results in mind we considered the many difficulties other researchers have encountered in attempting to
relate EEG to intelligence, cognition, and consciousness. We
had fortunately attended to several factors which seem to
have been neglected in the past: (1). We recorded EEG
while the subject was engaged in a task, rather than trying to
relate a "resting" EEG or averaged evoked potential to subsequent performance. (2). We selected cognitive tasks which
clinical evidence has shown to depend more on one hemisphere than the other, and which therefore would be associated with a predictable distribution of brain activity. (3).
We selected EEG-electrode placements on anatomical
grounds. A wealth of evidence suggests that temporal and
parietal areas of the brain should be the most functionally
asymmetrical, and the occipital areas the most similar. Unfortunately, occipital EEG leads have been used most often in
the past, probably because they are not as sensitive to eye
movement and muscle artifacts.

We then recruited ten new people for a formal study of
this phenomenon. The people were asked to write a letter, to
arrange wooden blocks to match a design, and, also, to per-

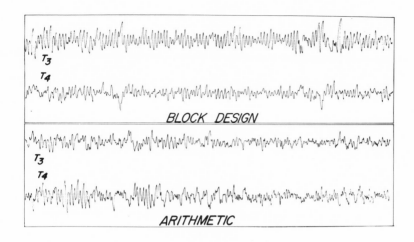

FIGURE 1B.

form mental versions of these tasks (mental letter writing and mental matching of forms). We analyzed the result in terms of the ratio of total right-hemisphere power to left-hemisphere power in both temporal and parietal pairs. We interpreted higher power in the EEG to mean more idling; a high ratio therefore meant more right-hemisphere idling and indicated a more active involvement of the left hemisphere in a task. Similarly a low ratio indicated a more active involvement of the right hemisphere. The results for the temporal leads are shown in Table 1 (the parietal leads are similar):

TABLE 1

Ratios: Right-Hemisphere Power/Left-Hemisphere Power

| SPATIAL TASKS | | VERBAL TASKS | |
Blocks	Mental forms	Written letter	Mental letter
0.83	0.90	1.01	1.02

These results confirmed our original ideas and observations, on a new set of subjects. The ratios were consistently higher for the verbal tasks than for the spatial, indicating more left-hemisphere involvement in verbal tasks, more right-hemisphere in spatial tasks.[3]

We later refined our measure, performing a Fourier (frequency) analysis on the EEG to determine how much of the effect was contributed by the alpha band, and how much by other frequencies. Considering the alpha band alone gives the results contained in Table 2.

TABLE 2

Right-Hemisphere Alpha/Left-Hemisphere Alpha

SPATIAL TASKS		VERBAL TASKS	
Blocks	*Mental forms*	*Written letter*	*Mental letter*
0.68	0.79	1.06	1.07

The spread between verbal and spatial tasks is greatest in the alpha band. The other frequencies show some asymmetry, but not as consistently as alpha. Analyzing the alpha alone yields a more sensitive index of the two hemispheres' activity—our resolution of task differences was increased two to five times compared with the previous analysis. The Fourier analysis allows us to chart the power at each frequency of the EEG, and to determine the points of maximum difference. One such graph of a Fourier analysis is shown in Figure 2. In the block design there is more alpha (8–12 cycles per second) in the left hemisphere than the right. The left-hemisphere (P_3) lead has a definite power peak at the center of the alpha band [10 cycles per second], while no such peak appears in the right-hemisphere lead

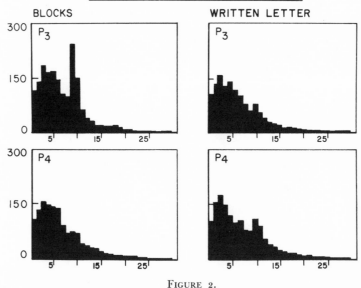

SAMPLE FOURIER POWER SPECTRA

FIGURE 2.

(P$_4$). In the writing task, the alpha peak in the left hemisphere is much lower than during the work with blocks, indicating the engagement of that half brain. During writing, the right hemisphere shows an increase in alpha compared to the period with the block design and is now greater than the left.

We are able, then, to distinguish two modes of consciousness, as they occur in normal people, using a simple scalp recording. This method enables us to index when a person is predominantly using the left hemisphere (and is presumably in an analytic mode), or using the right hemisphere (and is presumably in a holistic mode).

The next question we addressed was whether we could characterize different people as to their preferred mode of consciousness. At the same time, a new experiment afforded us the opportunity to confirm previous findings and to further refine our methodology.

It is a common observation that some individuals seem to use a verbal, analytic approach to problem solving while others use a spatial, holistic mode, even when this is not the optimum strategy. Our previous experiments show that the asymmetry in the EEG reflects the lateralization of verbal and spatial cognitive processes *within one person*. In this experiment we asked if this measure can be used to compare *two individuals*: for example, can we characterize one person as using the verbal-analytic mode more than another person? To test this hypothesis we selected people whose vocation would place primary emphasis on one of the two major cognitive modes. For the verbal-analytic group we chose eighteen lawyers and for the spatial-holistic group we chose seventeen sculptors and ceramicists (artists engaged in three-dimensional forms and images).

We refined an electrode cap from a previous design. Placements of EEG electrodes are ordinarily determined by hand measurement on the scalp, a process which is laborious and inaccurate. Our cap is made of light elastic and has plastic rings sewn over the standard EEG-recording points. It allows us to consistently locate the electrode sites on a subject, day after day, with little drudgery. The tips of the electrodes which contact the subject are fabricated from a dense plastic sponge. They are simply inserted in the holders on the cap and connected to the EEG amplifiers. The cap enables us to attach several electrodes to a subject quickly and accurately, and to easily change our selection of electrodes (Figure 3).

In this experiment our lawyers and artists were fitted with the cap, and sponge electrodes were inserted at three sites over the left hemisphere and at three over the right hemisphere. While the EEG was being recorded, they were asked to perform the block design previously described (Figure 4) and to trace a complex pattern viewed through a mirror (Figure 5), both presumably right-hemisphere tasks. Then the subjects were asked to write a description of a text from memory and to copy a similar text passage, presumably left-hemisphere tasks (Figure 6). These tasks were chosen to ob-

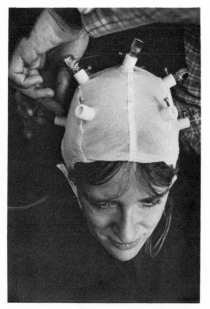

FIGURE 3.

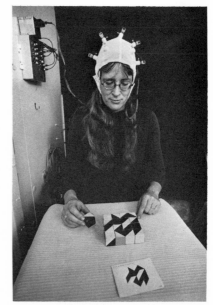

FIGURE 4.

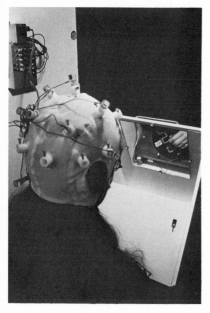

FIGURE 5.

FIGURE 6.

tain a set of verbal and spatial activities, one which required memory and one which did not. We chose electrode sites over the temporal, central, and parietal areas for the purpose of assessing within-hemisphere localization of memory and motor components of cognition. Although studies of cognitive deficits after brain lesions and injuries often show some anatomical specificity within each of the hemispheres, this was not evident on the EEG, as all of the three lead pairs yielded similar results. In considering these studies it is useful to recall that the EEG is a relatively crude indicator of brain processes, an average of the activity of millions of neurons.

We expected that the lawyers would show more of a "left-hemisphere" pattern on all tasks than the artists, that is, they would have consistently more right-hemisphere alpha and therefore higher right/left ratios. The results are summarized in Table 3. (We present, again, the temporal ratios. As noted the other two lead pairs were similar.)

TABLE 3

Right/Left Alpha Ratios for Lawyers and Ceramicists

| | SPATIAL TASKS | | VERBAL TASKS | |
	Blocks	*Mirror drawing*	*Writing from memory*	*Text copying*
Artists	0.76	0.75	1.05	0.91
Lawyers	0.79	0.75	1.19	0.96

This analysis of the task results confirms those of our previous experiment, showing a consistent difference between left- and right-hemisphere involvement in verbal and spatial processing, although our expectation of a large consistent ratio difference between vocational groups was not confirmed.

A second analysis did reveal a difference between the lawyers and artists. Instead of comparing the hemispheres to each other as previously with a right/left ratio, we examined the activity *within* each hemisphere. At each electrode site we formed the ratio of the alpha power on the spatial task to the verbal task. The greater the deviation from 1.00, the greater the change. This analysis reveals differences between the two groups in the extent to which the EEG of the right, the left, or both hemispheres changes with the task.

TABLE 4

Comparisons within Each Hemisphere

	BLOCKS/WRITING FROM MEMORY		MIRROR DRAWING/TEXT COPY	
	Left temporal	*Right temporal*	*Left temporal*	*Right temporal*
Artists	1.58	1.14	1.10	0.92
Lawyers	1.92	1.27	1.29	1.00

Table 4 shows that the group differ in their engagement of the left hemisphere; the lawyers show consistently greater change in left-hemisphere alpha than do the artists. Both groups show much smaller and more similar changes in the right-hemisphere leads.

These data also indicate that for both groups the left hemisphere tends to be more responsive to task demand—its alpha level changes more between tasks than the right hemisphere.

The lawyers, then, differ from the artists mainly in the use of their left hemisphere. The right hemispheres of both groups change less between tasks. Our within-hemisphere analysis is sensitive to these differences, although the right/ left ratio is not.

Conclusion

Now that we have established methods for determining the lateralization of cognitive function in the brains of normal people, we are able to study several additional research questions: the generality of lateral specialization of cognitive function in the population (so far we have studied right-handed males only), the role of lateral specialization in critical academic skills such as reading and arithmetic, the effect of social drugs on hemispheric interaction, and the possibility of training voluntary control over patterns of lateral asymmetry using EEG feedback. Our theoretical approach and experimental data provide a means of integrating research in many areas which touch on consciousness, e.g., clinical neurology, cognitive psychology, and electrophysiology.

Our development of EEG indicators of lateralized functions may enable ordinary individuals to achieve more precise control over their brain's activity. Instead of training nonspecific "alpha control" or "theta control," it may be possible to train functionally relevant *patterns* of activity.

The EEG measure may be used clinically to assess the brain localization of language. This would be useful to neurosurgeons who currently have to rely on anesthetizing each hemisphere by injection of barbiturates in the carotid artery. A less heroic method of determining language dominance would also have wide application in diagnosis and research in the areas of "minimal brain dysfunction," dyslexia, and developmental neuropsychology.

Our EEG studies provide potential methods of assessing preferences in cognitive mode. An individual's preferred cognitive style may facilitate his learning of one type of subject matter, e.g., spatial-relational, and hamper the learning of another type, e.g., verbal-analytic. A student's difficulty with one part of a curriculum may arise from his inability to change to the cognitive mode appropriate to the work he is doing.

Studies by Cohen[5] and by Marsh et al.[6] have indicated that subcultures within the United States are characterized by differences in predominant cognitive mode: the middle class more often employ the verbal-analytic mode, the urban poor are more likely to use the spatial-synthetic mode. This could result in a cultural conflict of cognitive style and may in part explain the difficulties of the urban poor children in a school system oriented toward the middle class. There seems to be a new recognition among educators of the importance of both modes of experiencing the world. Many new programs, for instance, emphasize helping verbal analytically oriented children to develop holistic-mode skills as well as helping spatially oriented children to make use of the traditional verbal-analytic materials. If our EEG feedback training project is successful, it may make it feasible to aid a child in entering both cognitive modes appropriately. With EEG feedback an individual may be able to learn to sustain a pattern of brain activity and the concomitant cognitive mode which is appropriate to reading and arithmetic on the one hand and painting and construction on the other.

This approach may also be of use in the study of cognitive development. Since brain injuries before the age of twelve rarely result in permanent aphasia (loss of expressive language) it is reasonable to suppose that the lateralization of cognitive functions is still in flux in young children after the acquisition of speech and even after the acquisition of written language. The maturation of the child's cognitive power may be paralleled by, and perhaps even depend upon, increasing lateral specialization of the brain with a resulting decrease in interference between cognitive systems. EEG measures of cognitive functioning might be powerful tools for mapping the course of this growth. These measures could be used in diagnosing disorders in cognitive development. For example, certain forms of dyslexia may be caused by interhemispheric interference. Perhaps "feedback" training to improve selective inhibition of the inappropriate cognitive mode would prove useful in therapy for these difficulties.

Our interest in the relationship of brain and conscious experience has also led to a consideration of philosophic and esoteric ideas. In an earlier essay in this volume Roger Bacon was quoted: "There are two modes of knowing, through argument and experience." These modes do seem to be the specializations of the two hemispheres in man. In our research we are studying the two modes of consciousness through the psychophysiology of normal people, in a new attempt to consider some of the most ancient ideas on the dichotomy of consciousness as they relate to the activity of the human brain.

5

ARTHUR DEIKMAN, M. D.

Bimodal Consciousness and the Mystic Experience

INTRODUCTION

The mystic experience is a psychological phenomenon that has largely been ignored by contemporary scientists. This situation is understandable. Scientists have waged a long battle to obtain their freedom from religious control, and mystical experiences are usually described within a religious idiom. It is natural that things mystical should be suspect and categorized as part of organized religion. In addition, the content and form of some types of mystical experience seem to give clear evidence of psychopathology. For this reason, the scientist may be tempted to dismiss all such reports as some type of hysteria or madness. Finally, and perhaps most important of all, to study the mystic experience requires participation on the part of the scientist so that he can stand outside of his customary mode of thought long enough to experience the different mode of consciousness involved in these phenomena. Such participant observation is not a part of the experimental model of contemporary science. Psychologists, in particular, have tended to model themselves after the eighteenth-century physicist, who believed he could be "objective" in observing the world. It is time to depart from this attitude. A careful reading of the classic mystical literature, as well as reports of psychedelic drug states, leads to the conclusion that the broad terrain of mystical phenomena contains within it lawful processes pertaining to a mode of consciousness as mature and as vitally practical as the one to which we are accustomed. In this paper, I will outline the evidence and logic supporting this assertion.

MYSTICAL PHENOMENA

The basic characteristic of mystical experience is the intuitive perception that we are part of a universe that is a unified whole. As William James and others have remarked, such an experience is usually accompanied by feelings of reverence and awe; it is highly valued and is felt to be a more direct perception of reality than is possible, ordinarily. Such an intuitive experience is called mystical because it is considered beyond the scope of language to convey.

Reports of mystical experiences encompass a wide area, from moments of joy and sensory enhancement not much different from ordinary consciousness, to states that are said to go beyond all images, ideas, and customary perceptual experiences. For descriptive purposes we can group these experiences into (1) untrained-sensate, (2) trained-sensate, and (3) trained-transcendent. "Untrained-sensate" applies to experiences occurring in persons not regularly engaged in meditation, prayer, or other spiritual exercises. Apparently, anyone can have a sensate-mystical experience.[1] Such states feature intense affective, perceptual, and/or cognitive phenomena that appear to be extensions of familiar psychological processes. Nature, drugs, music, and sex are frequent precipitating factors. William James cited the account of Trevor to illustrate such an experience:

> For nearly an hour I walked along the road to the "Cat and Fiddle," and then returned. On the way back, suddenly, without warning, I felt that I was in heaven—an inward state of

peace and joy and assurance indescribably intense, accompanied with a sense of being bathed in a warm glow of light, as though the external condition had brought about the internal affect-a-feeling of having passed beyond the body, though the scene around me stood out more clearly and as if nearer to me than before, by reason of the illumination in the midst of which I seemed to be placed. This deep emotion lasted, though with decreasing strength, until I reached home, and for some time after, only gradually passing away.[2]

In the same volume, James gave an example of someone undergoing chloroform anesthesia. This example is very similar to more contemporary accounts of persons using LSD 25 and related drugs:

I thought that I was near death; when suddenly my soul became aware of God, who was manifestly dealing with me, handling me, so to speak, in an intense, personal present reality. I felt him streaming in like light upon me. . . . I cannot describe the ecstasy I felt. Then, as I gradually awoke from the influence of the anesthetics, the old sense of my relation to God began to fade.[3]

Bucke, a physician, had a classical experience, occurring with no particular stimulus at all, arising from a state of quietude:

All at once, without warning of any kind, he found himself wrapped around as it were by a flame colored cloud. For an instant he thought of fire, some sudden conflagration in the great city, the next he knew that the light was within himself. Directly afterwards came upon him a sense of exultation, of immense joyousness accompanied or immediately followed by an intellectual illumination quite impossible to describe.[4]

The "trained-sensate" category refers to the same phenomena occurring in religious persons who have deliberately sought "grace" and "enlightenment" by means of long practice in meditation and religious discipline. The untrained-sensate and the trained-sensate states are phenomenologically indistinguishable, but the reports of trained mystics are usually expressed in the language of the religious system in which they are trained. As one might expect, a mystical experience occurring as a result of training, with the support and direction of a formal social structure and ideology, tends to have a more significant psychological effect. However, there are also accounts of spontaneous conversion experiences that are noteworthy for their influence on a person's life. It is typical of all mystical experience that it more or less fades away, leaving only a memory or longing for that which was experienced. The transensate or "enlightenment" experiences are said to have more permanent effects, but, even in those cases, training is continued for a long time until the person has "realized" the experience in his everyday life.

It would seem that mystical experiences form a progression when they occur as part of a specific spiritual discipline. Mystics such as St. John of the Cross and St. Teresa of Avila, commentators such as Poulain, and Eastern mystic literature, in general, divide the phenomena and stages through which mystics progress into a preliminary experience of strong emotion and ideation (sensate) and a higher experience—the ultimate goal—that goes beyond affect or ideation. It is the latter experience, occurring almost always in association with long training, that characterizes the "trained-transcendent" group. Poulain describes that state as follows:

> Then the spirit is transported high above all the faculties into a void of immense solitude whereof no mortal can adequately speak. It is the mysterious darkness wherein is concealed the limitless Good. To such an extent are we admitted and absorbed into something that is one, simple, divine, and illimitable, that we seem no longer distinguishable from it. . . . In this unity, the feeling of multiplicity disappears. When, afterwards, these persons come to themselves again, they find them-

selves possessed of a distinct knowledge of things, more luminous and more perfect than that of others. . . . This state is called the ineffable obscurity. . . . This obscurity is a light to which no created intelligence can arrive by its own nature.[5]

In "The Heart Sutra" what is apparently the same state is expressed as follows:

And no feeling, thought, impression, understanding, and no eye, ear, nose, tongue, body, mind, No form, sound, smell, taste, touch or thought. . . .[6]

UNDERSTANDING THE PROCESS

Classic mystical texts from widely varying cultures and times seem to prescribe the same basic psychological techniques for attaining the same basic alteration in consciousness. Considerations of space preclude listing enough examples to convey this impression as vividly as is justified, but, as an example, the instructions of Walter Hilton, a fourteenth-century Roman Catholic canon, are similar to those of Patanjali, a yogi from about the sixth century.

This vast literature can be summarized as follows: If a person wishes to achieve a special state that goes beyond the usual feelings and perceptions of ordinary life, a state in which the person perceives God or his own basic essence, it is necessary that he practice (1) a form of contemplative meditation and (2) renunciation.

Treating these instructions as technical psychological procedures, I then investigated contemplative meditation in a laboratory setting:[7,8]

CONTEMPLATIVE MEDITATION

Contemplation is a nonanalytic apprehension of an object or idea—nonanalytic because discursive thought is given up and with it the ordinary attempt psychologically to grasp or manipulate the object of attention. "Nondemanding attention" suggests the appropriate attitude. Ordinary thought is considered an interference; it hinders the direct contact that yields essential knowledge through perception alone.

A group of normal subjects, unfamiliar with meditation, were instructed to contemplate a simple blue vase according to the following instructions which I adapted from the yoga of Patanjali:

The purpose of the sessions is to learn about concentration. Your aim is to concentrate on the blue vase. By concentration I do not mean analyzing the different parts of the vase, or thinking a series of thoughts about the vase; but, rather, trying to see the vase as it exists in itself, without any connections to other things. Exclude all other thoughts or feelings or sounds or body sensations. Do not let them distract you, but keep them out so that you can concentrate all your attention, all your awareness on the vase itself. Let the perception of the vase fill your entire mind.

In the first series of experiments each subject performed the exercise for thirty minutes, during ten sessions spread over one month. I interviewed each subject immediately following each session and then analyzed the transcripts of the tape-recorded interviews. The subjects' experience of the vase changed as follows: (1) there was an increase in the vividness and richness of the vase image (e.g., they described it as "luminous," "more vivid"); (2) the vase seemed to acquire a life of its own, to be animated; (3) there was a decrease in the subjects' sense of being separate from the vase, occurring especially in those subjects who continued longest in the experiment (e.g., "I really began to feel, you know, almost as though the blue and I were merging or that the vase and I were. It was as though everything was sort of merging"); (4) a fusing of perceptual modes (e.g., "when the vase changes shape, I feel this in my body" and "I began to feel this light going back and forth").

As I discussed in an earlier paper,[7] these data are not easily explained by the usual concepts of projection or autohypnosis, sensory isolation, direct suggestion, or the influence of the demand expectations of the experimental situation. I hypothesized that these changes were a consequence of "deautomatization," an undoing of the usual ways of perceiving and thinking due to the special way that attention was being used. In particular, there seemed to be a deautomatization of the psychological structures that organize, limit, select, and interpret perceptual stimuli.

Deautomatization is a concept derived from Hartman's discussion of the automatization of motor behavior:

In well-established achievements they [motor apparatuses] function automatically: the integration of the somatic systems involved in the action is automatized, and so is the integration of the individual mental acts involved in it. With increasing exercise of the action its intermediate steps disappear from consciousness . . . not only motor behavior but perception and thinking, too, show automatization.

It is obvious that automatization may have economic advantages, in saving attention cathexis of consciousness in general. . . . Here, as in most adaptation processes, we have a purposive provision for the average expectable range of tasks.[9]

Gill and Brennan developed the concept:

De-automatization is an undoing of the automatizations of apparatuses—both means and goal structures—directed toward the environment. De-automatization is, as it were, a shake-up which can be followed by an advance or a retreat in the level of organization. . . . Some manipulation of the attention directed toward the functioning of an apparatus is necessary if it is to be de-automatized.[10]

The technique of contemplative meditation constitutes just such a manipulation of attention as is required to produce deautomatization. The percept receives intense attention while the use of attention for abstract categorization and thought is explicitly prohibited. Attention is *reinvested in perception*. Since automatization normally accomplishes the transfer of attention *from* a percept of action to abstract thought activity, the meditation procedure exerts a force in the reverse direction. Cognition is inhibited in favor of perception, since the active intellectual style· is replaced by a receptive perceptual mode. Automatization is a hierarchically organized developmental process, and one would expect a deautomatization to produce a shift towards a perceptual and cognitive experience, involving a mode developmentally preceding the more analytic abstract intellectual mode typical of present-day adult thought. The shift would be to a process lower in hierarchy, rather than a complete cessation of the particular function involved.

Heinz Werner studied the perceptual and cognitive function of children and members of primitive cultures. In discussing these studies, as well as the broader implications inherent in his studies of perceptual development, Werner stated:

> The image . . . gradually changed in functional character. It becomes essentially subject to the exigencies of abstract thought. Once the image changes in function and becomes an instrument in reflective thought, its structure will also change. It is only through such structural change that the image can serve as an instrument of expression in abstract mental activity. This is why, of necessity, the sensuousness, fullness of detail, the color and vivacity of the image must fade.[11]

He went on to describe the imagery and thought of primitive cultures and of children as (1) relatively more vivid and sensuous, (2) syncretic, (3) physiognomic and animated, (4) less differentiated with respect to the distinction between self and object and between objects, and (5) characterized by a lack of differentiation and a fusion of sense modalities. The phenomena that the subjects of my experiment reported fulfilled Werner's criteria completely, although the extent of the shift away from their normal consciousness was varied from one subject to the next. Their perceptual and cognitive changes were consistently in the direction of what Werner would describe as a more "primitive" organization.

I have been placing such terms as "primitive" and "regressive" in quotation marks for a particular reason. In an earlier paper I discussed the problem of what kind of "regression" might be involved and made reference to a frequently quoted passage by Wordsworth:

> There was a time when meadow, grove,
>   and stream,
> The earth, and every common sight,
> To me did seem
> Apparelled in celestial light,
> The glory and the freshness of a dream.

However, he may be confusing childhood with what is actually a reconstruction based on an interaction of adult associative capacities with the memory of the more direct sensory contact of the child. "Glory" is probably an adult product. Rather than speaking of a return to childhood, it is more accurate to say that the undoing of automatic perceptual and cognitive structures permits a gain in sensory intensity and richness at the expense of abstract categorization and differentiation. One might call the direction regressive in a developmental sense, but the actual experience is probably not within the psychological scope of any child. It is a deautomatization occurring in an adult mind, and the experience gains its richness from adult memories and functions now subject to a different mode of consciousness.[12]

It is a thesis of this paper that we have neglected the study of mystical experiences not only because of their association with organized religion, but because we have applied such prejudicial terms as "regressive," "immature," and "childish" to an area of function that may be of great value to us.

RENUNCIATION

Poverty, chastity, isolation, and silence are traditional techniques used in pursuing the mystical path. As dramatic as such techniques may be, they tend to obscure the fact that the renunciation sought is much more basic than merely modifying external behavior. For example, Walter Hilton prescribes a renunciation of thought:

> Therefore if you desire to discover your soul, withdraw your thoughts from outward and material things, forgetting if possible your own body and its five senses. . . . St. John calls for the banishment of memory:
> "Of all these forms and manners of knowledge the soul must strip and void itself, and it must strive to lose the imaginary apprehension of them, so that there may be left in it no kind of impression of knowledge, nor trace of aught so-ever, but rather the soul must remain barren and bare, as if these forms had never passed through it and in total oblivion and suspension. And this cannot happen unless the memory be annihilated as to all its forms, if it is to be united with God."[13]

Even more subtle and difficult is the statement of a contemporary Zen master that "[renunciation] . . . is not giving up things of this world, it is accepting that they go away."[14] At the time of the original meditation experiments I tended to understand renunciation as being a way to intensify the process of deautomatization by depriving perceptual and cognitive patterns of their usual stimulus nutriment, thereby helping to bring them into disuse and dysfunction. Also, it seemed as if renunciation would increase motivation, for having abandoned the world the mystic has no other hope of sustenance than his goal of enlightenment. However, at this point in my investigation I became a participant observer by undergoing meditation training under the auspices of the Zen Center of San Francisco. The meditation experience, coupled with visits to a Zen monastery, interviews with the Zen master, and reading of Buddhist literature, lead me to view renunciation in a different way.

Fundamentally, renunciation can be understood as relating to a change in *attitude*. It is a shift from *doing* to *allowing*, from grasping the world to allowing the world to enter us. It is the meditative attitude carried into everyday life. Ordinarily, we tend to categorize renunciation as virtuous, attributing various moral or holy qualities to it. However, my hypothesis is that the basic attitude or purpose of a human organism has a determining effect on its state of consciousness. From this point of view, renunciation is a practical, not a moral issue: your state of consciousness fits your intention, and renunciation changes intention.

TWO MODES

Let us think of a human being as an organism composed of components having both psychological and biological dimensions. These components have two basic modes of organization: an "action mode" and a "receptive mode." The action mode is a state organized to manipulate the environment. To carry out this purpose the striate muscle system is the dominant physiological agency. Base-line muscle tension is increased and the EEG usually features beta waves. Psychologically, we find focal attention, heightened boundary perception, object-based logic, and the dominance of formal characteristics over the sensory; shapes and meanings have a preference over colors and textures.

These attributes develop together. For example, as Piaget has shown, thinking develops in association with the manipulation and perception of objects, and object-oriented thought is associated with muscle activity, especially eye muscle activity.[15] Thus, we experience "effortful" thinking—reflecting the involvement of our muscle system. Likewise we can understand the perceptual characteristics of the action mode as providing what is needed for success in acting on the world. For example, a clear sense of self-object difference is necessary to obtain food. Similarly, a variety of psychological and physiological processes are coordinated and developed together in multidimensional unity adapted to the requirements of the task; i.e., manipulating the environment.

In contrast, the receptive mode is a state whose purpose is receiving the environment, rather than manipulation. The sensory-perceptual system is usually the dominant agency rather than the muscle system. Base-line muscle tension tends to be decreased, compared to the tension found in the action mode, and the EEG tends to the slower frequencies of alpha and theta. Psychologically we find that attention is diffuse, boundary perception is decreased, paralogical thought processes are evident, and sensory qualities dominate over the formal. These functions are coordinated to maximize the intake of the environment. As growth proceeds the receptive mode is gradually dominated, if not submerged, by a natural and culturally inforced emphasis on striving activity and the action mode that serves it. The receptive mode tends, more and more, to be an interlude between increasingly longer periods of action-mode organization. One consequence of this bias is that we have come to regard the action mode as the normal one for adult life and to think of the unfamiliar receptive states as pathological.

The pervasiveness of the action mode is evident when we consider that our language is its very essence. We use language to analyze, discriminate, and divide the world into pieces or objects which we can then grasp—psychologically and physically—in order to act upon them. The richness and subtlety of our language for any particular area of our lives reflects the extent to which we apply the action mode to that sector. For example, most of us have only one word for snow; if we are skiers we may have several. The Eskimo has many words that discriminate the varieties of snow conditions which he must take into account to survive. In some cases, the issue is not how many differences we have learned to detect but the mode of consciousness in which the experience takes place. "Love," for example, is represented for the average person by only one word. Yet, each of us probably has experienced many different varieties of that condition. We have not developed a rich vocabulary for love because it is experienced in the receptive mode; indeed, it requires the receptive mode for its occurrence. Similarly, color *experience* (rather than the use of color as a sign) requires the receptive mode and colors have only a relatively few names compared to the vast variety of hues to which we are sensitive. This is true even for the artist who *works* with, *manipulates*, and *makes* color objects and therefore has an expanded color vocabulary, compared to most people.

To illustrate these modes, let us consider some extreme examples. Imagine a cab driver in heavy traffic, struggling to get a passenger to the airport in time so that he may earn a large tip. He is intentionally engaged in maneuvering among the objects of his world and is focused on a future goal, trying as best he can to control what happens. He is not occupied with the color of the automobiles, the blueness of the sky, or the esthetic qualities of the streets and buildings, but sees only openings or blockades of traffic and notes only the colors of the stop lights. He sees the shapes and understands the meanings of the various objects flashing into his narrowed attentional field while at the same time part of his attention recalls alternate routes, and he scans his memory to remember the typical traffic flows. His base-line muscle tension is high and his EEG would probably show a desynchronized, fast voltage pattern.

In contrast, consider a monk, sitting in contemplative meditation in a garden. At that moment, his organism is oriented toward *taking in* the environment, a function that is performed via the receptive mode. If he is deeply into that mode, his state of consciousness may feature a marked decrease in the distinction between himself and his environment to the extent that he merges with it or has a nonverbal (ineffable) perception of unity, or both. Sensory experience dominates his consciousness, his muscles tend towards relaxation, and his EEG is likely to show alpha and theta waves. In contrast to the cab driver, he is not concerned with the future —he is letting whatever happens happen, while language and thinking are relinquished almost entirely.

During most of our lives what occurs is probably a mixture of the two modes or at least a fluctuation between them. For the majority of us, that fluctuation is heavily dominated by the action mode. However, it is not the presence or absence of physical activity per se that determines the mode. Rather, the underlying purpose or attitude seems to be crucial. For example, a monk working in a garden or lovers in sexual intercourse ideally would be very much given up to the receptive mode. The monk's relationship to his garden environment and the lovers' relationship to each other in the receptive mode is what Buber has described as the "I—Thou," in contrast to the "I—it" of the action mode.[16] However, if the monk in the garden is thinking about how soon he will attain enlightenment or if the lovers are concerned about their performance or are treating each other as fantasy objects, quite a different experience will result—in popular terms, it would be expressed as the difference between "making love" and "screwing." These are examples of the domination of different modes. An enlightened monk working in the garden may be trained to operate in the action mode only to the extent needed to perform the work, while allowing the receptive mode to play a prominent part in his conscious experience.

Thus, we are not talking about activity versus passivity as usually conceived, or about the secondary and primary processes of psychoanalytic theory. As I stated in an earlier discussion, "There is some similarity between aspects of the receptive mode and the cognitive style associated with primary process. The bimodal model, however, addresses itself to a functional orientation—that of taking in versus acting on the environment. The receptive mode is not a 'regressive' ignoring of the world or a retreat from it—although it can be employed for that purpose, but is a different strategy for engaging the world in pursuit of a different goal."[17]

RENUNCIATION AND MONASTIC TRAINING

With this discussion in mind, we can understand renunciation as a strategy to establish the receptive mode as the dominant orientation and to intensify its effects. In most spiritual disciplines a psychosocial system has been developed for use in a monastery or ashram, where technical exercises, communal living, and ideology are integrated to bring about change. It is instructive to look closely at one example of such a system; we can consider life in a Zen monastery of the Soto Zen sect. The basic principles of its operation are similar to those of other spiritual disciplines.

The Zen monastery teaches its students (monks) a state of acceptance and "nondiscrimination." This is accomplished by meditation, communal living, an ascetic way of life, and a supporting philosophy—Buddhism. There are different forms of meditation prescribed but the purest form is called *shikan-taza*, or "just sitting." A person performing *shikan-taza* is not supposed to do anything except to *be* sitting; trying to meditate better than the day before or trying to achieve enlightenment represent incorrect attitudes. Acceptance, rather than *doing*, is the basic instruction. Even intrusive thoughts or fantasies while meditating are not struggled against, but are treated as distractions that one must be patient with until they go away. The monk is told that if he is truly sitting, he is enlightened—to just sit, to just *be*, is enlightenment, itself.

The average person finds it very difficult to just sit and not do anything. When he tries it, he begins to realize how rigorously he has been trained to be busy, to solve problems, to make objects, to look ahead, to strive toward a goal. The sitting meditation may be regarded as an experiment in which the student explores what it is like when he does not respond to the usual commands of pain, anxiety, "boredom," or desires.

One effect of this meditation is to give the student the actual experience of having his ordinary sense of linear time change to something which might be described as timeless. For brief intervals, time can be felt to disappear—and anxiety with it. Likewise, the feeling of a personal self (the core dimension of the action mode) tends to become less vivid and, in some instances, may completely disappear.

The philosophical instruction that is given in lectures or, indirectly, through the chanting of religious texts, presents a theory that the world is one of constant change, composed of a basic nothing that takes an endless variety of forms but whose essence cannot be analyzed. In particular, the usual concept of death is taught to be an illusion. In this way, the most powerful force that orients us towards the future—the fear of death—is diminished.

The social systems of the monastery also undercut the action mode by minimizing material rewards. No one accrues profits; one day is very similar to the next. The food stays the same, there are few status rewards, and, thus, there tends to be nothing very concrete to "look forward to."

In these ways, the monastic system strikes at the attempt to grasp, to cling to, to strive for, to reach ahead and possess. The psychological importance of this is readily apparent. If we examine the content of our thinking, we can see that most of our energies are devoted to prolonging or bringing back a particular pleasure that we have had, often at the expense of enjoying the pleasure available at the moment. Operating in the action mode with an orientation towards the future, we tend to lose what is available to us in the present; for example, a man taking a pleasant walk on a beautiful spring day may be unhappy because he anticipates the ending of his vacation. In contrast, a monk or a yogi is taught to accept, to allow—rather than to be concerned with seeking pleasure or avoiding pain. To the extent that he succeeds in this reorientation, he establishes the groundwork for a mode of consciousness that the mystical literature describes as timeless, nondualistic, nonverbal, and completely satisfying. I propose that they are referring to a mode of organismic being that I have called the receptive mode, one that is natural to us, but seldom employed to its full potential.

THE RECEPTIVE MODE IN EVERYDAY LIFE

Although the foregoing discussion may seem to indicate that the receptive mode is the exclusive property of monks, in actuality, almost all of us make use of it to perform functions that we do not usually regard as esoteric. To take a very mundane example: trying to remember a forgotten name by a direct, conscious effort may yield nothing. In such a situation we typically remark, "It will come to me in a minute"— and it usually does. We stop struggling to remember and allow ourselves to be receptive. Only then does the name pop into awareness. Our shift in attitude—a change in strategy— permitted a latent function to be exercised. *Switching to the receptive mode permits the operation of capacities that are nonfunctional in the action mode.*

This principle is illustrated further when we consider a more important use of the receptive mode: to solve problems by means of creative intuition. Typically, there is an initial stage of struggling with the problem. A sense of impasse develops and the struggle is given up. Sometime later, while completely occupied with a less important activity, or perhaps waking from sleep, the answer suddenly appears. Often, it is in a symbolic or spatial form and needs to be worked over to make it coherent and applicable. In terms of the modal model, the process begins with the use of the action mode during the preliminary or preparatory stage. When progress is blocked, a shift takes place to the receptive mode. In that mode, our capacity for creative synthesis is able to function and the intuitive leap to a new configuration takes place. Then, we shift back to the action mode in order to integrate the new formulation with our previous knowledge and to communicate it to others.

For most people, the receptive mode probably has its most important function in sexual intercourse. The capacity for a deep and satisfying sexual experience is related to a person's ability to relinquish control, to allow the partner to penetrate both physical and psychological boundaries, and to stay focused in the present. Furthermore, sexual climax in persons who are thus able to "let go" is associated with heightened sensation, diffuse attention, and a decrease in the boundaries of the self (as in meditation); and in some cases, profound experiences occur that may be properly termed mystical.[1] In contrast, persons unable to give up their customary mode of active striving and control suffer a constriction of their sexual experience; pleasurable sensations, the release of tension, and feelings of closeness tend to be minimal or absent.

KNOWLEDGE

Mystics claim to have a direct, intuitive perception of reality, and that claim is a reasonable possibility. Studies in perception and developmental psychology indicate that we have exercised a significant selection process over the array of stimuli with which we are presented. For efficiency's sake, we have to pay attention to some things and not to others, and we automatize that selection process to such an extent that we cannot recover our perceptual and cognitive options. For that reason, mystical disciplines make use of a variety of means to bring about a deautomatization so that a new, fresh perception can occur. Perhaps when this deautomatization is combined with an increased capacity for receptive-mode function (as a result of "spiritual" training), the event of "awakening" to the awareness of one's true nature can then take place.

As in the case of creative intuition, descriptions of such "enlightenment" experiences indicate that they are sudden, involuntary, and present the "answer" in a flash. They tend to follow a long period of struggle and are often triggered by something of an irrelevant nature—the same pattern noticed for creative intuition. Furthermore, accounts of enlightenment often stress that additional work was needed before the new knowledge was fully "realized." We might say that it had to be integrated through use of the action mode. Thus, mystical "enlightenment" or "awakening" may be the result of a radical use of the basic creative process with which we are already familiar.

Whether or not mystical experiences yield knowledge about the world is an interesting question about which we have little data. However, LeShan has noted the striking correspondence between the cosmology of mystics and that of a number of modern physicists who also wrestle with questions about the essential nature of the universe.[18]

COMPLEMENTARY MODES

Although our conscious experience may seem to be a mixture of these different mode components, in a certain basic sense the modes appear to be *complementary*. The term "complementarity" was introduced by Niels Bohr to account for the fact that two different conditions of observations could lead to conclusions that were conceptually incompatible.[19] For example, in one set of experiments light behaved as if it were composed of discrete particles, while in another set of experiments light behaved as if it were a continuous wave. Bohr suggested that there was no intrinsic incompatibility between the two results because they were functions of different conditions of observation and no experiment could be devised that would demonstrate both aspects under a single condition. "Enlightenment" has been likened to an open hand. When you try to grasp it, you transform your open hand into a fist. The very attempt to possess it (the action mode) banishes the state because it is a function of the receptive mode. To put it in more modern terms, if you change your own organismic program from *intake* to *manipulate*, your functional characteristics will change at the same time.

CONCLUSION

Our ordinary mode of consciousness can be called the action mode, organized to manipulate the environment and featuring an acute consciousness of past and future time. Its basic reference point is the experience of a separate, personal self. In contrast, we have the capacity for a different organization—called the receptive mode—oriented towards the present, in which the personal self as a preoccupying orientation fades away and the world tends to be experienced as more unified and satisfying. As the action mode is used for problem solving and manipulating the environment, the receptive mode is used for receiving, for providing nutrition and satisfaction.

Which mode is better or "higher"? If we think in such terms, we are missing the point. We gain nothing by restricting our functions to one mode or the other. Rather, we need the capacity to function in both modes, as the occasion demands. There is a classical story that illustrates the exercise of this option: A man fell off the edge of a cliff and managed to grasp a small tree as he plunged downward. Looking up, he saw there was no way to climb back and looking down he saw jagged boulders waiting far below. He noticed that the roots of the tree were weakening and it was starting to come loose from the side of the cliff. Nothing could save him. At the same time, he noticed a small clump of wild strawberries lodged in a crevice of the rock. Holding on to the tree with one hand, he plucked a strawberry with the other and popped it into his mouth. How sweet it tasted!

What stands in the way of our making better use of this option, this nonordinary door to satisfaction, to creativity, to life in the present? It seems to me that the first barrier is our cultural bias that tells us that mystical states are unreal, pathological, "crazy," or "regressive"; it is a bias that declares the entire area to be "subjective" and, therefore, "unscientific." We have been indoctrinated neither to make use of nor to look closely at these realms. Without knowing it, under the banner of the scientific method, our thinking has been constricted. It is time that we made the receptive mode, and the experience which it engenders, a legitimate option for ourselves and for science. Having done so, we will be able to see more clearly the psychodynamic barriers that limit this option: defenses against relinquishing conscious control, defenses against the unexpected and the unknown, defenses against the blurring and loss of boundaries defining the self. We will be able to discriminate those instances in which the pathological or regressive are indeed present, but we will not miss seeing and exploring those phenomena that are truly mature and life promoting, of real practical value to us.

At this time in our history, our biological survival may depend on being able to utilize our receptive-mode function so that we will *experience* the basis for humanitarian values. We can recognize, theoretically, that selfless actions are necessary to regulate population, to deal with problems of pollution and resources, and end the possibility of a nuclear holocaust. However, the required virtues tend to be merely abstractions if they are not based on a personal realization of their validity, meaning, and importance. The action mode that pervades our civilization does not support selflessness; the receptive mode, ordinarily the specialty of mystics, does. From this point of view, mystics have been the guardians of a potentiality that has always been ours and that it is now time for us to reclaim. We can integrate this realm with our present knowledge, making it less exotic and less alien. By doing so, we can explore and regain a functional capacity that we may now need for our very preservation, as well as for the enlargement of our knowledge.

6

CHARLES T. TART, PH.D.

Discrete States of Consciousness

Introduction

I wish to begin by asking you to consider the following
question: do you *seriously* believe that your experience of
reading this book may be something you are dreaming? I
don't mean picky philosophical doubt about the ultimate nature of experience or anything like that; I'm asking whether
anyone in any seriously *practical* way thinks it might be a
dream he or she is experiencing now, rather than his or her
ordinary state of consciousness?

When lecturing I have asked this question of many audi-
ences, and I have seldom seen a hand go up, although occa-
sionally, with a California audience, someone will raise his
hand! If you took this question in the form of "How do you
know you're not dreaming now?" what you probably did was
to take a quick internal scan of the contents and quality of
your current experience and found that some specific elements of it, as well as the over-all pattern of your experience,
matched very well those qualities you have come to associate
with your ordinary waking consciousness, and did not match

the qualities you have come to associate with being in a dreaming state of consciousness.

I have asked this question in order to remind you experientially of a basic datum underlying my thesis, namely, that people sometimes scan the pattern of their ongoing experience and classify it as being one or another *state of consciousness*. This is the basic observation the concept of a state of consciousness starts from.

My purpose here is to share a conceptual framework I have been developing for several years about the nature of consciousness, and particularly about the nature of *states* of consciousness, with the hope that this theoretical framework will help our understanding of a vitally important area of knowledge, an area of knowledge that is currently in a condition that can only be called messy. Although the things we loosely call altered states of consciousness are often vitally important in determining human values and behavior, and although we are in the midst of a cultural evolution (or revolution, depending on your values) in which experiences from altered states of consciousness play an important part, our scientific knowledge of this area is just at its beginning. We have thousands of bits of unrelated data, a few relationships here and there, a small-scale theory for this and that, but mainly a mess. The theoretical framework I will develop attempts to give an over-all picture of this area and to guide future research in a useful fashion. In this symposium time limitations will force me to be very sketchy about many aspects of the theory that really ought to be presented in detail, and our rather vast ignorance in this area will force me to be sketchy about many more details.

The background ingredients of the theory are diverse, ranging from my personal experience, to experiential reports of experimental subjects and colleagues, to hints and ideas from the traditional psychologies of other cultures. To credit only those thinkers I am obviously indebted to, I should mention Carlos Castaneda, Arthur Deikman, Sigmund Freud, David Galin, George Gurdjieff, Ernest Hilgard, Thomas Kuhn, Carl Jung, John Lilly, Harold McCurdy, Gardner Murphy, Maurice Nicoll, Robert Ornstein, Peter Ouspensky, Claudio Naranjo, Ronald Shor, David Sobel, and Idries Shah. I shall emphasize a *psychological* approach to altered states of consciousness, as that is the approach I know best, and I believe it is adequate for building a comprehensive science of consciousness. The theoretical framework presented, however, is basically a *systems* approach to looking at consciousness, and can be quite easily translated into behavioral or neurophysiological terms. Those who feel more comfortable with such terminologies have free license to translate.

I shall speak rather abstractly in much of this paper to make clear what the conceptual framework is, but I am not speaking about an abstract topic. I am speaking about why your sons and daughters and students are using drugs or meditating; I am speaking about why some of you are meditating or trying psychedelics, about why some of you are feeling a diffuse dissatisfaction with your life—the framework I shall share with you can be usefully applied to an understanding of these things.

Ordinary Consciousness is a Construction

The basic point I shall try to make, as a prelude to discussing what *discrete states of consciousness* (d-SoCs) and *discrete altered states of consciousness* (d-ASCs) are, is that our ordinary consciousness is not at all a natural *given*, but a *construction*, and, in many important ways, a rather arbitrary construct. This is a difficult point to comprehend even on an intellectual level, much less a practical level, because, after all, we *are* our ordinary state of consciousness, and each of our egos tends to implicitly assume that the way *it* is is the natural, given standard of how an ego, a state of consciousness, *should* be. We shall work our way up to this conclusion more systematically.

I started this paper with an experiential reminder that we do make distinctions about states of consciousness. Let us now consider three categories of related assumptions underlying our theoretical structure, namely assumptions about awareness, assumptions about psychological structures, and assumptions about their interaction.

ATTENTION/AWARENESS

(1). We begin with a concept of some kind of basic *awareness*, some kind of basic ability to "know" or "sense" or "cognize" or "recognize" that something is happening. This is a basic theoretical and experiential given. We do not know scientifically what its ultimate nature is, but it is where we start from. I shall refer to this as *attention/awareness*, a term which implies a further basic given that we have *some* ability to direct this awareness from one thing to another.

This basic attention/awareness is something we can both conceptualize and experience as distinct from the particular *contents* of awareness at any time; i.e., to varying degrees, we can talk about attention/awareness as an experiential reality independent of any particular content of awareness. I am aware of a plant hanging in front of me at this moment of writing, and if I turn my head I'm aware of a chair. The function of basic awareness remains in spite of incredibly varied changes in its content.

(2). Another basic theoretical and experiential given is the existence, at times, of an *awareness of being aware, self-awareness*. The degree of self-awareness varies from moment to moment. At one extreme, I can be very aware that at this moment I am aware that *I* am looking at the plant in front of me. At the other extreme, I may be totally immersed in the sight of the plant, but I may not be aware of being aware of it. That is, there is an experiential continuum, at one end of which attention/awareness and the particular content of awareness are essentially merged,* while at the other end of the continuum there is awareness of being aware in addition to the particular content of awareness. In between are mixtures: at this moment of writing I am groping for clarity of the concept I am trying to express and trying out various word phrases to see if they do clarify and express it, and, in low-intensity flashes, I have some awareness of what I'm doing; but most of the time, I'm absorbed in this particular thought process. The lower end of the self-awareness continuum, relatively total absorption, is probably where we spend most of our lives, even though we like to credit ourselves with high self-awareness. The higher end comes to us more rarely, although it may be sought deliberately in certain kinds of meditative practices, such as the Buddhist Vipassana meditation.**

The ultimate degree of separation of attention/awareness from contents—allowing for self-awareness—that is possible in any final sense varies with one's theoretical position about the ultimate nature of the mind. If one adopts the conventional view that mental activity is controlled by the electrical–structural activity of brain functioning, there is a definite limit as to how far awareness can "back off" from particular contents, since that awareness is a product of the structure and contents of the individual brain. This is a psychological manifestation of the principle of relativity.[1] Although the feeling of being aware of being aware has an "objective" quality to it, this conservative position would say that this objectivity is only relative, for the very function of awareness itself stems from and is shaped by the brain activity that it is attempting to be aware of.

A more radical view, common to the spiritual psycholo-

---

* Something that we can only know retrospectively.

** It may be that self-awareness is actually an all-or-none phenomenon, usually occurring in very brief flashes. Variations in the density of these flashes over time may give the "illusion" of a continuum. Further observation is needed here.

gies,[2] is that basic awareness is not just a property of the brain but is at least partially something from "outside" the workings of the brain. Insofar as this is true, it is conceivable that most or all content associated with brain processes could potentially be "stood back" from so that the degree of separation between content and attention/awareness, the degree of self-awareness, is much higher than in the conservative view.

Whichever ultimate view one takes, what is psychologically important for studying consciousness is that the degree of separation of attention/awareness from content, the degree of self-awareness, varies considerably from moment to moment.

(3). Attention/awareness can be volitionally directed to *some* extent. If I ask you to become aware of the sensations in your left knee now, you can do so. But few would claim anything like total ability in directing attention. If you are being burned by a flame, it is well-nigh impossible to direct your attention/awareness to something else and not notice the pain at all, although this can be done by certain people and by many more people in certain states of consciousness. As with the degree of separation of attention/awareness from content, the degree to which we seem able volitionally to direct our attention/awareness also seems to vary. Sometimes we can direct our thoughts according to a predetermined plan easily, at other times our mind seems to wander with no regard at all for our plans.

Stimuli and structures (we shall deal with structures below) attract or capture attention/awareness. When you are walking down the street and there is the sound and sight of an accident with a crowd suddenly gathering, your attention is attracted to it. Similarly, ongoing mental activity, activated structures, tends to attract any loose, contentless attention/awareness and bind that attention/awareness to it. This attractive pull may outweigh volitional attempts to deploy attention/awareness elsewhere.

For example, we worry over and over about a particular

problem, and are told that we're just wasting our energy going around in circles and should take our attention off the problem. In spite of wishing to do so, it may be almost impossible to direct our attention elsewhere.

The ease with which particular kinds of structures and contents capture attention/awareness will vary with the state of consciousness and the personality structure of the person; e.g., things that are highly valued or are highly threatening capture attention much more easily than things which bore us. Indeed, we could partially define personality in terms of the structures which habitually capture a person's attention/awareness.

(4). Attention/awareness constitutes the major phenomenal energy of the consciously experienced mind. "Energy" is here used in the most abstract sense of the term, i.e., the ability to do work, the ability to make something happen. Attention/awareness is, then, an energy in the sense that structures having no effect on consciousness at a given time can be activated if given attention, or structures may draw attention/awareness energy automatically, habitually, as a function of personality structure, thus keeping a kind of low-level, automated attention in them all the time (these are our long-term desires, concerns, phobias, blindnesses), or attention energy may inhibit particular structures from functioning. The selective redistribution of attention/awareness energy for desired ends is the essence of innumerable systems that have been developed to control the mind.

(5). The total amount of attention/awareness energy available to a person varies from time to time, but there may be some fixed upper limit on it for a particular day or other time period. Some days we simply can't concentrate well no matter how much we desire it; other days we seem to be able to focus clearly, to use lots of attention to accomplish tasks. We talk about "exhausting" our ability to pay attention, so phenomenally the total amount of attention/awareness energy available may be fixed for various time periods under ordinary conditions.

Let us now look at basic theoretical postulates about the mental/psychological structures which utilize the energy of attention/awareness.

STRUCTURE

(6). This theory postulates that the mind, from which consciousness arises, consists of a myriad of structures.

A psychological *structure* refers to a relatively stable organization of component parts which performs one or more related psychological functions.

We infer (from "outside") the existence of a particular structure by observing that a certain kind of input information reliably results in a certain kind of transformed output information under typical conditions. For example, we ask someone "How much is fourteen divided by seven?" and he answers "Two." After repeating this process, with variations, we infer the existence of a special structure or related set of structures we might name something like "arithmetical skills." Or we might infer (from "inside") the existence of a particular structure when, given certain classes of experienced input information, we experience certain transformed classes of output/response information. For instance, I overhear the question about fourteen divided by seven and observe that some part of me automatically "says" two, so I infer an arithmetical-skills structure as part of my own mind.

We hypothesize that structures generally continue to exist even when they are not active, not functioning, since they operate again when appropriate activating information is present. I again know that fourteen divided by seven is two, even though I stopped thinking about it for a while.

The emphasis here is on the structure forming something that has a recognizable shape, pattern, function, process. Ordinarily in dealing with the structure, we are interested in its over-all properties as a complete structure, as a structured system, rather than in the workings of its component parts. Insofar as any structure can be broken down into sub-substructures, one can do finer analyses ad infinitum; e.g., the "arithmetical-skill" structure could be broken down into adding, subtracting, multiplying, dividing substructures. Such microscopic analyses, however, may not be relevant to understanding the properties of the over-all system, the state of consciousness, that one is working with. The most obvious thing that characterizes an automobile *as a system* is its ability to move passengers along roads at high speed, and doing a metallurgical analysis of its spark plugs is not very relevant to understanding its primary functioning and nature. Our concern then is with psychological structures that show functions useful to our understanding of consciousness. Such structures might be given names like sexual needs, social coping mechanisms, language abilities, etc.

Note that there may be structures of such complexity that we are unable to recognize them as structures, only seeing component parts and never seeing how they all work together.

(7). A psychological structure may show variation in the intensity and/or the quality of its activity, both over-all and in terms of its component parts, but still retain its basic patterns, its basic Gestalt qualities, its basic system function, and so remain recognizably the same. A car is usefully referred to as a car whether it is driving at five miles an hour or twenty-five miles an hour, whether it is red or blue, whether the original spark plugs have been replaced by spark plugs of a different brand.

(8). Some structures are essentially permanent, they cannot have their important aspects of functioning modified in any significant way, they are biological/physiological givens. They are the "hardware" of our mental system, to use an analogy from computer programing; they are programs built into the machinery of the nervous system.

(9). Some structures are mainly or totally given by an

individual's particular developmental history; i.e., they are created by, programed by, learning, conditioning, and enculturation processes that the particular individual undergoes. This is the "software." Because of the immense programability of human beings, most of the structures that interest us, that we consider particularly *human*, fall in this software category.

(10). Permanent structures create limits on and add qualities to what can be done with programable structures; i.e., the hardware puts some constraints on what the software can be. The physiological parameters constituting a human being place some limits on his particular mental experience, his possible range of programing.

Our interest today is in relatively permanent structures, ones that are around long enough for us conveniently to observe and study—hours or weeks or years—but all the theoretical ideas in this paper should be applicable to structures which are not long-lasting, even though their investigation may be more difficult.

Structures, then, are hypothesized explanatory entities based on either experiential, behavioral, or psychological data.

Let us now consider the interaction of attention/awareness and structures.

INTERACTION OF STRUCTURE
AND ATTENTION/AWARENESS

(11). Many structures function totally autonomously of attention/awareness. Such are basic physiological structures like our kidneys. We infer their integrity and nature as structures from other kinds of data, as we do not have any direct awareness of them.* Such structures do not utilize attention/

---

* We should be careful about any a priori statements that certain structures must be out of awareness. Data from the rapidly developing science of biofeedback, and traditional data from yoga and other spiritual disciplines,

awareness as an energy, but as some other form of physiological activating energy. Structures which cannot be observed by attention/awareness are of incidental interest to the study of consciousness, except for their context-forming, indirect influences on other structures that are accessible to conscious awareness.

(12). Some structures must use a certain amount of attention/awareness energy in order to: (a) be formed or created in the first place (software programing); and/or (b) operate; and/or (c) have their operation inhibited; and/or (d) have their structure or operation modified; and/or (e) be destructured, dismantled. We shall now call these *psychological structures* when it is important to distinguish them from structures in general. Thus many structures require some amount of attention/awareness energy for their initial formation—the energy originally required to learn arithmetical skills is an excellent example. Once the knowledge or structure we call arithmetical skills is formed, it is usually present only in inactive, latent form. When an arithmetical question is asked, attention/awareness is put into that particular structure, and we exhibit, experience, arithmetical skills. If our original learning, structuring, programing was not very thorough, a fairly obvious amount of attention/awareness energy is necessary to use this skill. Once the structure has become highly automated and overlearned, only a small amount of attention/awareness energy is experienced as being needed to activate and run the structure; we solve basic arithmetic problems with little awareness of the process involved in so doing.

Note that while we have distinguished attention/awareness and structure for reasons of analytical convenience and to be true to certain experiential data, ordinarily we infer the exis-

---

should remind us that many processes long considered totally outside of conscious awareness can be brought to conscious awareness with appropriate training.

tence of *activated* mental structures, i.e., we get data about structures when the structures are functioning, utilizing attention/awareness energy.

(13). Although we postulate attention/awareness energy as capable of activating and altering psychological structures, as being the "fuel" which makes many structures run, observation indicates that affecting the operation of structures by the volitional deployment of attention/awareness energy is not always easy. We may attempt to alter a structure's operation by attending to it in certain ways with no effects, or even with effects contrary to what we desire. We may wish a certain structure would stop operating and try to withhold attention energy from it, and yet find the structure continuing to attract attention/awareness energy and to function. The reasons for this may be twofold.

First, if the structure is (at least partially) operating on kinds of energy other than attention/awareness energy, such as physiological energy, it may no longer be possible to deactivate the structure with the amount of attention/awareness energy we are able to focus on it. Second, because automatization is so thorough and overlearned and/or because the structure has very vital connections with the reward and punishment system of the personality, such that there are secondary gains from the operation of the structure in spite of our apparent complaints, the amount of attention/awareness energy we can use to try to alter the structure's functioning is not sufficient. Indeed, it seems clear that in dealing with ordinary people in ordinary states of consciousness, the amount of attention/awareness energy subject to conscious control and deployment may be quite small compared with some of the relatively permanent investments of energy in certain basic structures comprising the individual's personality and his adaptation to the consensus reality of his culture.

(14). Insofar as the amount of attention/awareness energy available at any particular time has a fixed upper limit, some decrements should be found when too many structures draw on this energy simultaneously. If the available attention/awareness energy is greater than the total used by the simultaneous activation of several structures, no decrements will occur.

(15). Once a structure has been formed and is operating, either in isolation or in interaction with other structures, the attention/awareness energy required for its operation may be automatically drawn on either intermittently or continuously; i.e., the personality and "normal" state of consciousness are operating in such a way that attention is repeatedly and automatically drawn to the particular structure. Personality may be partially defined as the set of interacting structures (traits) that habitually are activated by attention/awareness energy. A person may not realize that his attention/awareness energy is being drawn to a particular structure, unless he develops the ability to deploy attention in an observational mode, the self-awareness mode, and sees this. As mentioned earlier we must distinguish the case where the structure learns to operate with some different kind of energy than attention/awareness energy. Some of these latter kinds of structures may still be capable of deautomatization with the proper deployment of attention/awareness energy to them, even though this process may be difficult.

There is a fluctuating but generally large drain on attention/awareness energy at all times by the multitude of automated, interacting structures whose operation constitutes our personality, our "normal" state of consciousness, our perception of and interaction with consensus reality. Because the basic structures comprising this are activated most of our waking life, we do not perceive this activation as a drain on attention/awareness energy but simply as the "natural" state of things. We have become habituated to it. The most important kind of data supporting this observation comes from reports of the effects of meditation, a process that in many ways is a deliberate deployment of attention/awareness, that takes attention away from its customary structures and either puts it in nonordinary structures or tries to maintain it as a relatively pure, detached awareness. From those kinds of experience it can be seen that attention/awareness energy must be used to support our ordinary state of consciousness. Furthermore, from these kinds of experiences of great clarity, the automatized drain of attention/awareness energy into habitually activated structures is seen as attentuating the clarity of basic awareness, so ordinary consciousness is seen as blurred and dreamlike.

Let us now consider the interaction of structures with each other.

INTERACTION OF STRUCTURES WITH STRUCTURES

(16). Although the interaction of one structure with another structure depends on the structures being activated by attention/awareness energy, this interaction is modified by an important limitation, namely that *individual structures have various kinds of properties* which also limit and control their potential range of interaction with one another. That is, structures are not "equipotential" with respect to interacting with one another, but have important individual characteristics.

Consider that any structure has one or more ways in which information can be put into it, and one or more ways in which information is given out by the structure.* We can say in general that in order for two structures to interact they must have either a direct connection between them or some connections mediated by other structures; their input and

---

* For more complex structures, we should probably also distinguish between inputs and outputs that we can be consciously aware of with suitable deployment of attention/awareness, between inputs and outputs which we cannot be consciously aware of but which we can make inferences about, and between inputs and outputs which are part of feedback control interconnections between structures, which we cannot be directly aware of.

output information must be in the same kind of "code" so information output from one "makes sense" to the input for another; the output signals of one structure must not be so weak that they are below the threshold for reception by the other structure, nor must the output signals of one structure be so strong that they overload the input of the other structure.

Now let us consider ways in which psychological structures may *not* interact, with a possible example of each. First, two structures may not interact if there is no direct or mediated connection between them. I have, for example, structures involved in moving the little finger on my left hand and sensing its motion, and I have structures involved in sensing my body temperature, say, in telling whether I have a fever or a chill. Although I am moving my little finger vigorously now, I can get no sense of having either a fever or a chill from that action. Those two structures seem to be totally unconnected.

Second, two structures may not interact if the codes of output and input information are incompatible. My body, for example, has learned to ride a bicycle. While I can sense that knowing in my body, in the structure that mediates my experience of riding a bicycle when it is actually in action, I cannot verbalize it; the nature of the knowledge encoded in that particular structure does not code into the kinds of knowledge that constitute my verbal structures.

Third, two structures may not interact if the output signal from one is too weak, below the threshold for affecting another. I may be quite angry with someone and arguing with him. During the argument a "still small voice" in me is telling me that I am acting foolishly, but I have very little awareness of this still small voice, and it cannot affect the action of the structures involved in feeling angry and arguing.

Fourth, two structures may not interact properly if the output signal from one overloads the other. I may be in severe pain during a structural integration session, for instance, and I "know" (another structure tells me) that, if I could relax, the pain would be lessened considerably, but the structures that are involved in relaxing are so overloaded by the intense pain that they cannot carry out their normal function.

Fifth, two structures may also be unable to interact properly if the action of a third structure interferes with them. An example is neurotic defense mechanisms. Suppose, for instance, your boss is a despicable character and constantly humiliates you. Yet part of your personality structure has a strong respect for authority, and you believe in yourself as a very calm person who is not easily angered. Now your boss is humiliating you, but instead of feeling angry, the "natural" consequence of the situation, you are polite and conciliating, and don't feel the anger. A structure of your personality has suppressed certain possible interactions between other structures.

Let us now look at the case of smoother interaction between structures. We may, for instance, have two structures interact readily and smoothly with one another to form a composite structure, a system whose properties may be additive properties of the individual structures, as well as acquiring Gestalt properties unique to the combination. Or, two or more structures may interact with one another in such a way that the total system alters some of the properties of the individual structures to various degrees, and so we have a system formed which has Gestalt properties, but not necessarily simple additive properties of the individual structures. We may also have unstable interactions of two or more structures where they in some sense compete for energy, and we have a kind of unstable shifting relationship in the composite system.

All of these considerations about the interactional structures apply to both hardware and software structures. For example, two systems may not interact because their basic neural paths, laid down in the hardware of the human being, cannot make such interaction possible. Or two software structures may not interact because in the enculturation, the programing of the person, the appropriate connections were simply not created.

One could look at all the classical pyschological defense mechanisms in these system terms, but space precludes that here.

Remember that in the real human being we probably usually have many structures interacting simultaneously with all the above factors for facilitating or inhibiting interaction to various degrees at various points in the total system formed.

The basic point of this postulate, to summarize, is that while the interaction of structures is affected by the way attention/awareness energy is deployed, it is also affected by the properties of individual structures.

Developmental Construction of Ordinary Consciousness

We have postulated basic components of consciousness, viz. attention/awareness and structures. Let us look at how our ordinary, or so-called "normal," state of consciousness is formed, how attention/awareness and structures form a *system*.

THE SPECTRUM OF HUMAN POTENTIALITIES

A helpful concept that I learned from anthropology is the idea of the *spectrum of human potentialities*. Figure 1 diagrams this idea. By virtue of being born a human being, having a certain kind of body and nervous system (the hardware), and functioning in the general environment of spaceship Earth, a very wide variety of behaviors and experiences are *potentially* available to you. These may include running a four-minute mile, being able to learn mathematics, various kinds of esthetic experiences, etc.

But any individual human being will only develop a small fraction of his total human potentialities because he is born into a particular culture at a particular place and time, has certain parents, relatives, peers, and teachers, and has various "random" events happen to him. A culture can be looked at as the creation of a group of programers who have (implicitly) agreed that certain human potentialities are beneficial and should be developed, and have set up a society, a system of interlocking relationships, to select these potentialities out of the total spectrum of human potentialities, to develop them, and to program them, to various degrees. These selections are shown by the pointed arrows in Figure 1. The same culture also knows about certain other human potentialities, but considers these as undesirable or bad, and actively blocks their development. How many of you, for example, were given basic instruction in grade school on how to go into a trance state so your mind could be possessed by a friendly spirit that might teach you interesting songs and dances? Not many, I warrant! In fact, if you had started developing that potential on your own and were foolish enough to talk to your teacher or your parents about it, I suspect you would have been very actively discouraged from any further development! Yet in many other cultures, this kind of human potential is highly valued.

Figure 1 shows two cultures which have made different selections from the spectrum of human potentialities. Sometimes the potentials cultivated overlap between cultures. All cultures, for instance, teach people some kind of language. Yet what is "good" and cultivated by culture A may not be cultivated at all by culture B, or even be actively rejected as an undesirable trait by the second culture.

Note further that any given culture not only selectively develops some potentials and actively inhibits others, but the culture simply doesn't know about a very large variety of other potentials. Thus they are not developed as a result of

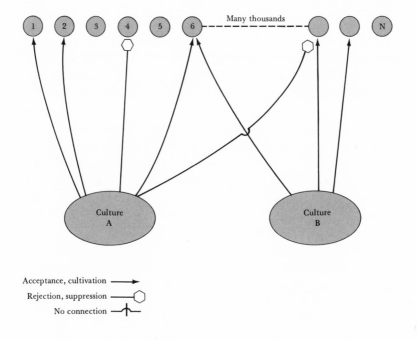

FIGURE 1. Spectrum of Human Potentialities.

ignorance and lack of use, rather than inhibition. Eskimos, for example, discriminate and have separate words for seven different kinds of snow. We do not have such fine discriminations in our culture, as it does not occur to us that we need to, or could, make such fine discriminations.

Within the cultural framework there will be further limitations depending on particular circumstances, and there are also genetic differences in each individual's inheritance, but the cultural limitations and selections, the programing of the software, seem much more obvious than the genetic ones at this point.

Figure 2 summarizes the process of enculturation, of "maturation" (given culturally relative standards for maturity). We come into the world with a range of human potentialities that include (1) a basic capacity for awareness; (2) fixed structures (hardware) such as a skeleton, musculature, digestive organs, which *must* develop if we are to be a functioning organism; (3) fixed structures which *may* develop, given the necessary conditions (which may not happen in a particular culture), such as Jung's archetypal experiences; and (4) a very wide range of highly programable structures from which the culture will develop a number, such as the potential to speak English. The selective development and inhibition of potential structures by cultural, physical, and random factors, and the automatization of attention/awareness energy into the system built from these structures produces a "normal" consciousness for a given culture, an individual who perceives reality and acts "appropriately" within the culturally sanctioned framework (consensus reality). Enculturation is an enormously complex process, but space forbids my going into detail.

FIGURE 2. Enculturation.

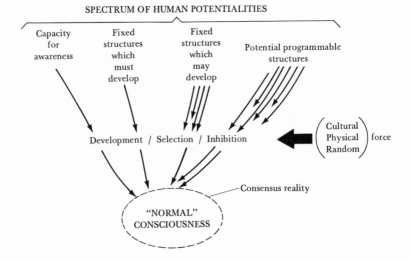

SPECTRUM OF HUMAN POTENTIALITIES

SPECTRUM OF EXPERIENTIAL POTENTIALITIES

This same concept of the spectrum of human potentialities can be extended to a spectrum of consciousness potentialities, or experiential potentialities. Look again at Figure 1, but change the label "culture" to "state of consciousness." This illustrates how two different cultures have different systems comprising their ordinary states of consciousness, but let us view it as showing two possible organizations, systems, states of consciousness, in one individual. In his ordinary state of consciousness, the culturally "normal" state, represented by the circle at the lower left, a given individual is able to have certain kinds of experiences, use certain kinds of psychological skills. Some other kinds of mental skills are actively inhibited in his ordinary state of consciousness. Many other experiential potentials that the individual was born with were simply never developed and so are not available in his ordinary state of consciousness. Some of these may still be latent, waiting for the right stimulus to turn them into usable structures, others may no longer be developable due to disuse. An individual is simultaneously the beneficiary and the victim of his culture's choices from the spectrum of experiential potentialities.

Now, using the idea of the states of consciousness as implying an over-all active organization of consciousness, an interacting system of structures activated by attention/awareness energy, it may be possible for this same individual to change into an *altered* state of consciousness, a new active organizational patterning of his consciousness, and in this second state he may be able to tap and use certain of these potentialities or structures that are unavailable in his ordinary state of consciousness. This is represented by the lower right-hand circle in Figure 1. The availability of new human potentials, new modes of functioning of consciousness in altered states of consciousness is a prime reason for our interest in them, especially if one does not feel that one's ordinary state of consciousness allows optimal functioning.

Just as two cultures may develop some common human potentialities, most of the altered states of consciousness that we know much about do share some psychological structures with our ordinary state of consciousness. For example, a person usually speaks his native language, both in his ordinary state of consciousness and in an altered state of consciousness.

Discrete States of Consciousness

TERMINOLOGICAL PROBLEMS

As we start to focus on states of consciousness, note that a first problem in studying this area is terminological. The terms "states of consciousness" and "altered states of consciousness" have now become very popular. I share a certain amount of guilt in having helped to popularize them by editing the book *Altered States of Consciousness*.[3] As a consequence of becoming popular, however, they are frequently used in such a loose fashion as to mean almost nothing in particular. Many people now use the term state of consciousness, for example, to simply mean whatever is on their mind. So if I pick up a water tumbler and look at it, I am in a water-tumbler state of consciousness, and if I now touch a table, I am in a table state of consciousness, and if I now touch the top of my head, I'm in a top-of-my-head state of consciousness, etc. Then an *altered* state of consciousness simply means that what you are thinking about or experiencing now is different or altered from what it was a moment ago. I would prefer to stick with statements about the experience of the moment, or what's on your mind right now for that sort of use, and try to rescue the concepts of state of consciousness and altered state of consciousness for scientific use by introducing the terms "discrete state of consciousness" (d-SoC) and "discrete altered state of consciousness" (d-ASC). I have given the basic theoretical postulates for defining these crucial terms, but, rather than proceeding with the definition, I would first like to look more directly at certain kinds of experiential data that lead up to the concepts by a slightly different route.

MAPPING EXPERIENCE

Suppose, as psychologists, students of the mind, we believe that an individual's experience (and/or behavior) could be adequately described at any given moment if we knew all the important dimensions along which experience varies, and could assess the exact point along each dimension that an individual occupied at a given moment. Each dimension might be the level of functioning of a psychological structure. That is, we presume we have a multidimensional map of psychological space, and by knowing exactly where the individual is in that psychological space we can adequately describe his experiential reality. This is a generally accepted theoretical idea, but, of course, it is very difficult to apply in practice because there may be many psychological dimensions important for an individual's experience at any given moment. We may be able to assess only a small number of them, and/or an individual's position on some of these dimensions may change even as we are busy assessing the value of others. Nevertheless, it is an ideal to be worked toward, and we shall assume that we can do this with some adequacy.

To further simplify for discussion, let us assume that what is important about an individual's experiences can be mapped along only two dimensions, so we can draw a nice graph. Figure 3 represents such a mapping. Ignore the illustrative labels on the two dimensions for a moment, and simply consider them two dimensions of psychological experience. Each small circle represents an observation, at a single point in time, of where a particular individual was in this two-dimensional psychological space. In this particular example, we have taken a total of twenty-two measures at various times.

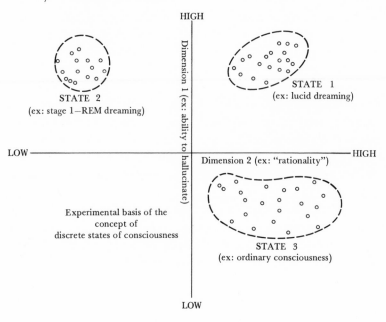

FIGURE 3. Mapping Experience.

The first thing that strikes us about this individual is that his experiences seem to fall in three distinct clusters, and that there are large gaps between these three distinct clusters. Within each cluster this individual shows a certain amount of variability, but he has not had any experiences at points outside the defined clusters. This kind of clustering in the plot of an individual's location at various times in experiential space is precisely what I mean by a *discrete state of consciousness.* To put it another way, it means that you can be in a certain region of experiential space and show some degree of variation within that space, but then to transit out of that space you have to cross a "forbidden zone,"* where you ei-

---

* "Forbidden zone" applies under ordinary circumstances of a stable personality, and shall not be taken in too absolute a way.

ther cannot function and/or cannot have experiences and/or cannot be conscious of having experiences, before you find yourself in a discretely different experiential space. It is the quantum principle of physics applied to psychology:[1] you can be either here or there, but there is no way you can be in between.

There are transitional periods between some d-SoCs, and we will deal with them in more detail later. For now, being in a d-SoC means that you are in one or another of these three distinct regions of psychological space shown in Figure 3.

Now let's concretize this example and refer to the labels I have put on the two axes in Figure 3. Let's call dimension 1 one's ability "to image" or "hallucinate," varying from a low, at one extreme, of literally just "imagining" that one sees something outside oneself but not having anything corresponding to a sensory perception at all, to the high extreme of this continuum, where what one images has all the qualities of "reality," of an actual sensory perception. Let's call dimension 2 one's ability to be "rational," one's ability to think in accordance with the rules of some logic or other. We won't concern ourselves with the cultural arbitrariness of "logic" here, but simply take it as a given set of rules. One could vary from a low of making many mistakes in the application of this logic, as on days when one feels rather stupid and has a hard time following what people say, to a high of following the rules of the logic perfectly, feeling sharp as a tack, as they say, with one's mind working like a precision computer.

Now we can give names of d-SoCs to the three clusters of data points on the graph. *Ordinary consciousness* (for our culture) is shown in the lower right-hand corner. It is characterized by a high degree of rationality, and a relatively low degree of imaging ability. We can usually think without making very many mistakes in logic, and most of us have images with some mild sensory qualities, but they are far less intense than sensory perception. Notice again that there is variability within the state we call ordinary consciousness. My logic may be more or less accurate, my ability to image may vary somewhat, but this all stays in the ordinary, habitual range.

At the opposite extreme, we have all experienced a region of psychological space where rationality may be very low indeed, while ability to image is quite high. This space is represented by the cluster of points in the upper left quadrant of Figure 3. This is ordinary dreaming, where we create the entire dream world, image it; it seems real, yet we often take considerable liberties with rationality.

The third cluster of data points defines a particularly interesting d-SoC, *lucid dreaming*. This is the special kind of dream, named by the Dutch physician Frederick van Eeden, in which one feels as if one "wakes up" in terms of mental functioning *within* the dream world; i.e., one feels as rational and in control of one's mental state as in an ordinary state of consciousness, but one is still *experientially located within the dream world*.[4] Here we have a range of rationality at a very high level and a range of ability to image also at a very high level.

A d-SoC, then, refers to a particular region of experiential space as we have shown here, and adding the adjective "altered" simply means that, with respect to some state of consciousness (usually our ordinary state) that we use as a base line, we have made the "quantum jump" to another region of experiential space, another d-SoC. The quantum jump may be both *quantitative* in the sense of structures functioning at higher or lower levels of intensity and *qualitative* in that structures in the base-line state may cease to function, previously latent structures may begin to function, and the system pattern may change. The graphic presentation of Figure 3 doesn't lend itself to expressing qualitative changes, but they are more important than the quantitative ones.

The qualitative pattern difference between two discrete states of consciousness is emphasized in Figures 4 and 5. Here various structures are shown connected into a pattern in different ways. The latent pattern, the discrete altered state of consciousness, is shown in lighter lines on each figure. The two states share many structures or functions in common, yet the organization is distinctly different.

FIGURE 4. Representation of a d-SoC as a configuration of structures/subsystems forming a recognizable pattern. Light lines and circles represent *potential* interactions and potentialities/structures/subsystems not used in the base-line d-SoC.

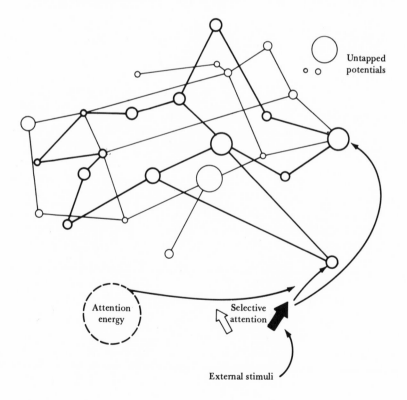

Now let's go into even more detail. I shall define a d-SoC for a given individual as a unique *configuration* or *system* of psychological structures or subsystems. The structures show some variation in the way in which they process information, or cope, or have experiences within one or more varying environments. The structures operative within a d-SoC comprise a *system* where the parts, the psychological structures,

FIGURE 5. Representation of a d-ASC as a new configuration of structures/subsystems, a new Gestalt. The configuration of the base-line d-SoC (Figure 4) is shown in light lines and circles. Although there is some overlap of connections and structures/subsystems, a distinctly new pattern has emerged, and different human potentials are used in different ways to form a new system, the d-ASC.

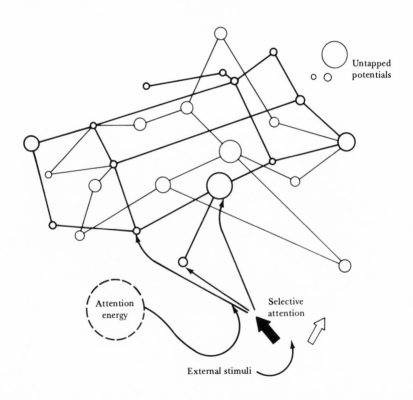

interact with each other and stabilize each other's functioning by means of feedback control, so that the *system*, the d-SoC, maintains its overall patterning of functioning within a varying environment. That is, the parts of the system that comprise a state of consciousness may change over various ranges individually, but the general configuration, the over-all pattern of the system, remains recognizably the same.

The way to understanding a d-SoC, therefore, depends both on understanding the nature of the parts, the psychological structures or subsystems that comprise it, and on taking into account the Gestalt, pattern properties, which arise from the over-all system and which are not an obvious result of the functioning of the parts.* For example, a list of an individual's traits and skills may tell me a little, but to understand him I need also to consider the pattern that emerges from their organization into a personality, into a "normal" state of consciousness.

To make this more concrete, let's go back to the question I asked at the beginning of this chapter about whether you thought this might all be a dream rather than your ordinary state of consciousness. To conclude that what was happening then was real (I hope you concluded that!), you may have looked at the functioning of your component structures: my reasoning seems sound, sensory qualities are in the usual range, body image seems right, criticalness is intact, etc., and concluded that since these component structures were in the range you associate with your ordinary state of consciousness. that that's where you were, that's the condition you were in. Or you may have simply felt the Gestalt pattern of your functioning, without bothering to check component functions, and instantly recognized it as your ordinary pattern. Either

---

* A further practical limitation in our understanding of d-SoCs is that they must have some reasonable stability over time: we can imagine d-SoCs that would only hold a particular pattern for a fraction of a second, but this would be too short for us to make any useful kinds of observations of their properties. The ones we are beginning to have any knowledge about can all last from periods of minutes to hours to lifetimes.

way, you scanned data on the functioning of yourself as a system, and categorized the system's mode of functioning as its ordinary one.

Let me make a few further comments about the discreteness of different states of consciousness and the quantum leaps between them.

DISCRETENESS OF STATES
OF CONSCIOUSNESS

First, it should be realized that the concept of d-SoCs, in its common-sense form, did not come from the kind of precise mapping along psychological dimensions that I have sketched in Figure 3. Rather, the immediate experiential basis for the concept is usually Gestalt-pattern recognition, the feeling that "this condition of my mind feels *radically different* from some other condition, rather than just an extension of it." The experiential mapping is a more precise way of saying this.

Second, for most of the d-SoCs that we know something about, there has been very little or no mapping of the transition from the base-line state of consciousness to the altered state. Little has been done, for example, in examining the process whereby one passes from an ordinary state of consciousness into the hypnotic state,* although for most subjects the distinction between the well-developed hypnotic state and their ordinary state is very marked. Similarly, when one begins to smoke marijuana, there is a period of time during which one is in an ordinary state of consciousness and smoking marijuana, and then, later, one is clearly "stoned," i.e., in a d-SoC we call marijuana intoxication. The only study of this is a preliminary survey that Joseph Fridgen and I carried out,[5] in which we asked experienced marijuana users about the transition from the one state to the other. Our main finding was that users almost never bothered to

---

* Some preliminary psychoanalytic investigations carried out by Gill and Brenman are of interest here.[6]

look at the transition, either being in a hurry to get into the intoxicated state or being in social situations that didn't encourage them to observe what was going on in their minds.

So, in general for d-SoCs, we don't really know what the size and exact nature of the quantum jump is, or, indeed, whether it might in some cases be possible to effect a continuous transition between two regions, thus making them extremes of one state of consciousness rather than two discrete states.

Because the science of consciousness is in its infancy, I am forced to spend too much time talking about what we don't know and the difficulties in research, so let me balance this a little by describing a study that has done some mapping of the transition between two discrete states of consciousness, viz. between ordinary waking consciousness and sleep. Vogel, Foulkes, and Trossman,[7] using electroencephalographic (EEG) indices of the transition from full awakeness (alpha EEG pattern with occasional rapid eye movements, REMs) to full sleep (stage 2 EEG, in Figure 6, no eye movements), awoke subjects at various points in the transition process, asked for reports of mental activity just prior to awakening, and also asked routine questions about the degree of contact with the environment the subjects felt they had just before awakening. They fitted this experiential data into three "ego states." In an *intact ego state*, the content of experience is "plausible," i.e., it fits consensus reality well, and there is little or no loss of reality contact. In the *destructuralized ego state*, content is bizarre and reality contact is impaired or lost. In the *restructuralized ego state*, contact with reality is lost but the content is plausible by consensus-reality standards.

Figure 6 shows the frequency of these three ego states, or states of consciousness, with respect to psychophysiological criteria. The psychophysiological criteria are arranged in the order in which transition into sleep ordinarily takes place. It can be seen that the intact ego state is associated with alpha

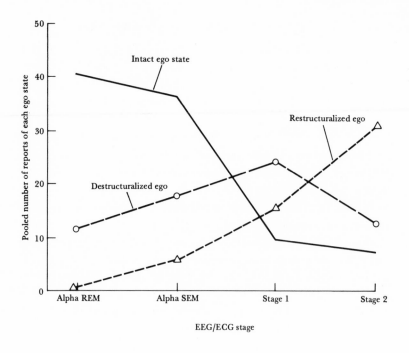

FIGURE 6. Ego States During Sleep Onset.

and REM or alpha and SEM (slow eye movement), the de-structuralized state mainly with stage 1 EEG, and the re-structuralized state with stage 2 EEG. But there are exceptions in each case. Indeed, a finer analysis of the data shows that the sequence of intact ego → destructuralized ego → restructuralized ego almost always holds in the experiential reports; it is a more solid finding than the association of these ego states with particular physiological stages. Some subjects start the intact → destructuralized → restructuralized sequence earlier in the EEG sequence than others. This is a timely reminder that trying to equate psychological states with physiological indicators often leads to fallacies. But the main point to note here is the orderliness of the transition sequence from one discrete state to another. This experiment uses a crude level of measurement compared to what we need, but it is a good start.

Stabilization of a Discrete State of Consciousness

The basic function of a d-SoC is to successfully cope with the world, or external environment. It is a tool, a sensing tool, that interprets what the world is, and plans and executes strategies for dealing with the changing world. A good tool should not break easily when applied to the job: the system of structures and attention/awareness energy that constitutes our state of consciousness should maintain its integrity in coping with the changing world it was designed for. So a d-SoC is a *dynamic* system, parts of it changing all the time, that maintains the over-all pattern/organization that is its nature. Let us look at the stabilization process.

There are at least four major ways of stabilizing a system that constitutes a d-SoC. They are analogous to the way people control one another. If you want someone to be a "good citizen": (1) you keep him busy with the activities which constitute being a good citizen, so he has no time or energy for anything else; (2) you reward him and make him feel good for carrying out these activities; (3) you punish him if he engages in undesirable activities; and (4) you try to eliminate opportunities for engaging in undesirable activities. The following discussion can apply both to the stabilization of the d-SoC as a whole and of the individual structures/subsystems within that d-SoC.

LOADING STABILIZATION

The first major type of stabilization is what we might call ballasting, or *loading*, to use an electrical analogy. In electrical ballasting, you impose a large electrical load on an output circuit that draws on the power resources sufficiently so that very high voltages cannot occur; the power supply lacks the capacity to produce them, given the load. Loading in general refers to any kind of an activity that draws most of the energy of the system so that the system cannot swing into the use of undesirable excesses of energy. A load may also store energy, giving the system inertia which prevents sudden slow downs. Psychologically, loading means keeping a person's consciousness busy with the desired types of things, involving such a large proportion of the attention/awareness energy normally produced in the desired activities that not enough is left over to have the potential for disrupting the system's operation. As don Juan told Carlos Castaneda, the ordinary, repeated, day-to-day activities of people keep their energy so bound within a certain pattern that they cannot become aware of nonordinary realities.[8]

For example, right now in your ordinary state of consciousness, which I presume you are all still in, a number of things act as loading stabilization processes. For one thing, the stable physical world around you and the invariant relationships in it give you a pattern of input which constantly stimulates you in expected patterns that you are used to. If you push your hand against the chair you're sitting in, it feels solid, just as it always has felt. If you push it again, it will still feel solid, and so on. You can depend on the lawfulness of the spectrum of experience we call "physical reality." But, if the next time you pushed on the chair, your hand started passing *through* the material of it, I expect most of you would be rather surprised or alarmed and immediately begin to suspect that this was not your ordinary state of consciousness!

As a second example, your body (and your internalized body image) is another source of stabilization via loading. Every morning when you wake up you have one head, two arms, and two legs. Although the exact relationship of the parts of your body to one another change, as do internal feelings within it, the changes are all within a well-learned range. If you suddenly felt half of your body starting to disappear, this would again make you ask whether you were in your ordinary state of consciousness.

As a third example, if you move your body, it has a certain feel to it; the kinesthetic feedback information about the relations of parts of your body and muscle tensions as you move is also within an anticipated range. Since we move around a lot, this loads us with familiar input. If your arm suddenly felt three times as heavy as usual as you lifted it, this might disrupt your ordinary state of consciousness.

As a fourth example, we have a constant internal thinking process going on, constant internal chatter, which runs through familiar and habitual associative pathways and keeps us within our ordinary state of consciousness. We think the kinds of things that please us, we feel clever as a result of thinking them, feeling clever makes us relax, feeling relaxed makes us feel good, feeling good reminds us that we are clever, etc. This constant thinking, thinking, thinking, thinking, thinking also loads our system and is very important in maintaining our ordinary base-line state of consciousness.

NEGATIVE-FEEDBACK STABILIZATION

The second major type of stabilization is what we might call *negative feedback*. Particular structures or subsystems sense when the rate or quality of operation of other subsystems goes beyond certain preset limits and then begin an active correction process. This correction signal might be conscious as, for example, when thought processes stray into certain areas that are taboo for that person and anxiety results. The anxiety then functions to alter subsystems to re-stabilize them within the acceptable range.

You may not be conscious of a particular feedback correction process. For example, you may be lost in thought and suddenly find yourself very alert and listening to your environment, although not knowing why. A sound signal that indicated a potentially threatening event may have occurred very briefly, and while not intense enough to be consciously perceived was enough to activate a monitoring mechanism that then sent out correction signals to bring the system of consciousness back within optimal (for dealing with the threat) range. This kind of negative feedback stabilization, then, essentially measures when a system's or structure's operation is going beyond acceptable limits and initiates an act of correction of this, reducing the deviation.

POSITIVE-FEEDBACK STABILIZATION

The third kind of stabilization processes is what we might call *positive feedback,* and consists of structures or subsystems that detect when acceptable activity is going on and then stimulate the emotional reward systems, thus making us feel good when we do that particular activity. We may not be particularly conscious of the "feeling-good" quality. However, we like to maintain and repeat the rewarded activity. During the formation of our ordinary state of consciousness in childhood, we are greatly rewarded by parents, peers, and teachers for doing various socially approved of acts, and, insofar as most of our socially approved actions are initiated by socially approved thoughts, we then internalize this reward system and feel okay simply by engaging in the thoughts or actions that have been rewarded earlier.

Let's illustrate how feedback stabilization can work. You are driving home late at night and you're rather sleepy. Driving carefully was an active program in your ordinary state of consciousness, but now, because of fatigue, your mind is drifting toward a hypnogogic state even though you're managing to hold your eyes open. Hypnogogic thoughts are sometimes very *interesting*—we assume they are now—so your mind starts pursuing some further. Because the integrity of the ordinary state is now beginning to be disrupted, you do not make an appropriate correction as the car begins to drift over toward the shoulder of the road. You run off the shoulder, narrowly avoiding an accident, which jars you back to full wakefulness. Sometime in the future the same circumstances occur again, but now some part of your mind notes the fact that your thoughts are becoming very interesting in that hypnogogic way *and* the fact that you are driving, and, via the emotional subsystem, sends a feeling of anxiety or alarm through you which immediately activates various subsystems toward highest physical-world-survival priority modes of operating, and reinstates full consciousness. Thus we have an example of a state of consciousness learning that certain processes indicate that part of its system is going beyond a safe limit of functioning; the error information then does something to restore that ordinary range of functioning, i.e., it exerts feedback control. You may or may not have had much direct experience of the feedback process per se.

LIMITING STABILIZATION

A fourth way of stabilizing a d-SoC can be called *limiting* stabilization. Here we interfere with the ability of some subsystems or structures to function in a way which might destabilize the ongoing state of consciousness, i.e., we limit the ability of certain subsystems, should they become activated, to destabilize the state. It is analogous to spoiling the airflow over a rudder; the rudder then loses most of its ability to alter the flight of the aircraft.

An example of limiting stabilization would be one of the effects of tranquilizing drugs; many of them seem to blunt emotional responses of any sort, limit the ability of certain subsystems to produce strong emotions. Insofar as strong emotions can be important forces in destabilizing an ongoing state of consciousness, this limiting thus stabilizes the ongoing state. Sufficient limiting of crucial subsystems could thus not only stabilize any d-SoC that did not need those subsystems, but it would make it impossible to go into a d-ASC that required functioning of the limited subsystems.

Note that when dealing with a system as multifaceted and

complex as a d-SoC, at any given instant there may be several of each of the four types of stabilization activities going on. Further, any particular action may be complex enough to function as more than one of these kinds of stabilization simultaneously. For example, suppose I have taken a drug and for some reason decide I don't want it to affect my consciousness. I may begin thinking *intensely* about personal triumphs in my life. This can stabilize my ordinary state of consciousness by loading it, absorbing most of my attention/awareness energy into that activity so that it can't drift off into things that would help the transition to an altered state. It would also act as positive feedback, making me feel good and thereby increasing my desire to keep up this kind of activity.

Note that the terms positive feedback and negative feedback, as used here, do not necessarily refer to consciously experienced good or bad feelings. Negative feedback refers to a correction process initiated when a structure or system starts to go, or has gone, beyond acceptable limits, a process of decreasing deviation. Positive feedback is an active reward process occurring when a structure or subsystem is functioning within acceptable limits, enhancing functioning within those limits.

Subsystems Comprising Discrete States of Consciousness

The general picture of a particular d-SoC, made up of a certain number of psychological structures or subsystems, each with its own characteristics, interacting with each other in a certain pattern, can be developed in detail in many ways. The subsystems are structures, or groups of related structures, that are activated by attention/awareness and/or other sorts of energy. The particular number and kind of subsystems necessary for an adequate system description will vary greatly with the focus of the particular problem and with the theorists handling the problem. What might look like a *basic* psychological structure or subsystem to one theorist may be seen as capable of being broken down into simpler structures by another. My own theorizing at this time calls for ten major subsystems, plus an undetermined number of latent psychological functions which may come into operation in a d-SoC. My current choice of subsystems is based on what I know about the general kinds of variations one sees in many d-SoCs, as conceptualized by the kind of psychological knowledge currently available. I want to mention them briefly just to put a little flesh on the skeleton I have been building. Each of the subsystems I shall discuss is a *convenient* subsystem in terms of summarizing present knowledge, but certainly would be susceptible to finer analysis if we had more data. Someday each of these subsystems will be treated as a system itself and analyzed into finer subsystems.

Figure 7 shows ten major subsystems: *exteroceptors, interoceptors, input processing, memory, sense of identity, evaluation and decision making, motor output, subconscious, emotion,* and *time sense.* The heavy arrows represent major information-flow pathways within the system. The extra-large arrows represent input from the external world or body, or output to the external world or body. The dashed, heavy arrows represent important information-flow routes that are only inferential rather than directly experiential in our ordinary state of consciousness. The lighter, hatched arrows represent feedback control pathways between various psychological systems, i.e., information-flow routes which do not necessarily represent consciously experienced information but the influences of one subsystem on another which keep them operating within a range appropriate for maintaining the over-all d-SoC.

I have not attempted to show all major information-flow routes; to do so would produce much too messy a diagram. Thus the figure shows only some of the major and more ob-

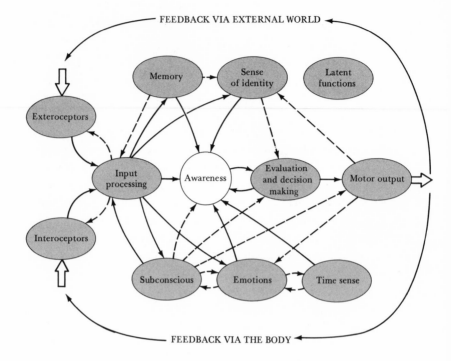

FIGURE 7. Subsystems Comprising States of Consciousness.

vious information- and feedback-flow routes. An oval for latent functions is shown as not connected to other psychological subsystems, to illustrate the latent structures that may be activated or constructed as we go to a d-ASC. The dotted circle labeled *awareness* is the "ghost in the machine," the psychological function of basic attention/awareness, the function which extends into or activates structures or subsystems.

I shall very briefly say something about the nature of each subsystem and the range of variation it may show in various d-ASCs.

Exteroceptors refer to our classical sensory organs for perceiving energies in the external world, while *interoceptors* refer to those senses for perceiving the conditions of our own body. Deliberately altering input to exteroceptors and interoceptors is used in most techniques for inducing d-ASCs. There may be changes in the functioning of interoceptors or exteroceptors resulting from the induction of an altered state, although these are usually insignificant compared to other subsystem changes.

We know very little about the functioning of exteroceptors and interoceptors in isolation, psychologically speaking, because they each feed their information into one of our most important psychological subsystems, *input processing*. This is the vast collection of perceptual learnings that makes our perception highly selective. It is the process that throws away ninety-nine per cent of the sensory data actually reaching us and passes on to awareness only instantaneous abstractions of what is "important" in the stimuli reaching us at any time. Changes in input processing, such as deautomatization[9] of this abstracting process, occur in many altered states and account for the reports of enhanced vividness and beauty of perception. Information flow can also be cut to almost nothing, producing phenomena like analgesia.

All of these psychological subsystems are here being given convenient names for what are related collections of structures and functions, as is obvious in the case of *memory*. It is a great oversimplification to speak as if we have one unitary memory. We have a large number of specialized memories for handling different kinds of information. In various altered states, memory function may be grossly deteriorated, may be greatly enhanced, or may shift in style of functioning, as when memories start being recalled as vivid visual images rather than verbal abstractions about stored data, or when state-specific memory functions.

The psychological subsystem labeled *sense of identity* is that collection of psychological functions that we might call the ego or the sense of my-ness. It is a *quality* that gets added to other information within our state of consciousness, rather than necessarily being information itself, a quality that, because we value our egos, calls for special handling of information that it is attached to. For example, if I live in a large city and look out of the window and see some kids smashing a parked car, I might be relatively blasé and feel minor indignation at the lawlessness of our times, but not inclined to do anything about it. If, with further information coming out of input processing and memory, I recognize. that it is *my* car that they are smashing up, the same information that a car is being smashed up now acquires an entirely new priority and emotional tone, to put it mildly! The sense of my-ness or egoness is highly variable in d-ASCs, and may go from a low of zero, where everything is perceived simply as information and there is no ego on the scene, to a high where the self becomes extended to include other people, other events, or even the whole universe.

The subsystem labeled *evaluation and decision making* refers to our cognitive processes, the various learned (and perhaps partially innate) rules and procedures we use for analyzing and working with information according to one or more kinds of logic. This subsystem can not only work more or less efficiently in d-ASCs, but the particular logics with which it works can be deliberately altered. For example, in hypnosis a subject can be given an axiom that there is no such thing as the number five, that it is a meaningless concept, and he then evolves a new arithmetic taking this axiom into account. Or Gestalt qualities may become more important than verbal components in deciding whether two things are "equivalent" in reasoning.

The subsystem labeled *subconscious* includes the classical Freudian and Jungian unconscious but is more comprehensive than that, including many of the qualities that Frederick Myers, for example, would have identified as the subliminal self. It refers to all those psychological functions which are not directly available to consciousness in an ordinary state of consciousness but which we hypothesize as being active in order to account for observable conscious behavior and experience. In some d-ASCs, processes which were subconscious in the ordinary state, i.e., that we only *hypothesized* to exist, may become directly possible to experience.

The subsystem labeled *emotion* refers to all of our various emotional feelings. In d-ASCs a variety of changes may take place, such as stimuli triggering different emotions than they normally do, or emotional intensity being much greater or less than it ordinarily is. Starting from our ordinary state of consciousness, *extreme* intensities of emotion can disrupt it and induce altered states, so we shall eventually have to discriminate discrete emotional states of consciousness.

The psychological function labeled *time sense* refers to the general feeling we have for the rate of flow of time and the structuring of experience in terms of psychological time. It may be based at least partially on internal biological rhythms, as well as on cues from external events. In various d-ASCs, time sense may speed up, slow down, seem to stop, or events may even seem to happen totally out of their normal order, with the future preceding the past. I stress that this is a *psychological* time sense we're talking about, an internally *generated* concept of time, a construction, rather than simply some kind of physiological or psychological process that merely mirrors clock time.[10] Whether we want to consider clock time more "real" is an interesting question.

We may eventually call this subsystem a time–space sense to handle the psychological construction of a spatial as well as a temporal framework for experience.

The final subsystem diagramed in Figure 7 is *motor output*, which refers to both our voluntarily controlled skeletal muscles and various internal effects on our body of taking various kinds of actions, such as glandular secretions. Motor output may be inhibited, unaffected, or enhanced in various altered states.

Predictive Capabilities
of the Theory

Having given our abstract structures more definite shape in terms of current knowledge, and having available a convenient descriptive system, we can now see how the theoretical system can be used to make testable predictions about d-SoCs. The basic predictive operation is a cyclical one. The first step is to observe the properties of structures/subsystems as well as possible with the current state of knowledge. The second step involves organizing the observations to make better theoretical models of the nature of the various structures/subsystems that have been observed; and, from these models, the third step is to predict how the structures/subsystems can and cannot interact with each other under various conditions. Fourth, these predictions are tested by looking for or attemping to create d-SoCs that fit or do not fit these improved structure/subsystem models, and the models are evaluated. Then the beginning step above is repeated, and further altering or refining of the models continues.

Basically what the theoretical system herein proposed does is provide a conceptual framework for organizing knowledge about states of consciousness and a process for continually improving our knowledge about the structures/subsystems. The ten subsystems sketched above are crude concepts at this state of our knowledge, and should eventually be replaced with more precise and a larger number of more basic subsystems; then, also, their possibilities for interaction to form systems must be explored.

I have given little thought, to date, to making predictions based on the current state of the theory. The far more urgent need, at this chaotic state of the new science of consciousness, is to organize the mass of unrelated data we have to make it manageable. I believe that most of the data now available can be usefully organized in the conceptual framework I am presenting today, and that the framework is a clear step forward in organizational comprehensibility. The *precise* fitting of the available mass of data into this theoretical framework will be a work of years, however.

One obvious prediction of this theory is that because of the differing properties of structures, restricting their interaction, there is a definite limit to the number of stable d-SoCs. Ignoring enculturation, we can say that the number is large but limited by the hardware endowment of man in general. The number of possible states for a particular individual is even smaller because of further limits and qualities of structures brought about by enculturation.

I will briefly illustrate the kind of more specific predictions that can be made by (falsely) assuming our current knowledge of the subsystems discussed above is rather good. I would regard the following prediction as illustrative and designed to sharpen our thinking, rather than as one likely to have good validation.

I would predict that in an intact human being you cannot have a d-SoC that shows the following three concurrent characteristics: (1) feelings of intense sexual arousal via the interoceptors; (2) feelings of greatly enhanced perception via the exteroceptors of the external world, such as richer colors, enhanced depth relationships; and (3) almost zero feeling from the body itself via the interoceptors. This prediction is based on the observation that various d-SoCs sometimes involve an almost total cutting off of input from the environment (via the exteroceptors) and/or from the body (via the interoceptors) or, at the opposite extreme, apparent enhancement of sensory qualities, but seldom both together. This suggests that input processing as a subsystem has a very limited capacity selectively to use a larger number of both kinds of inputs at one time. Especially since high sexual arousal usually involves increased attention to the body generally (a structure/function built into the hardware?) as well as specifically sexual areas, the characteristics of input processing would seem to preclude a generally increased flow of sensation from both extero- and selected interoceptors and a simultaneous blocking of most impulses from the body.

I have deliberately chosen a tricky example here to illustrate the complexity of the system as a whole. It is known, e.g., that sexual excitement can make one selectively unaware of *some* parts of the body, such as injured parts. Furthermore, there are yogic disciplines that involve the experiential conversion of sexual feelings into a feeling of "energy" that leads to an altered state of consciousness, but this usually involves loss of most external sensation, and is a very "internal" trip. But the highly selective combination of intense sexual excitement, psychedeliclike enhancement of sensation through the exteroceptors, and zero feeling from the body itself seems to be beyond the capacity of input processing per se as a subsystem, or beyond the interaction potentials of combined systems.

I stress again, though, that our need today and the primary use of this conceptual system is useful organization of data, not prediction. Prediction and hypothesis testing will come into their own in a few years as our understanding of structures/subsystems sharpens.

Individual Differences

Now we must turn our attention to a methodological pitfall that has seriously slowed psychological research in general, as well as research on states of consciousness. This is the lack of adequate recognition of individual differences.

Lip service is paid to individual differences all the time in psychology courses, but in practice the degree of respect is quite different. Individuality is something that is relegated to the clinical psychologists' domain, and everyone "knows" clinical psychologists practice more of an art than a science. As scientists, who have been caught up in the all too human struggle for prestige, we ape the physical scientists for whom individual differences are not of great significance, and the search is for general, "fundamental" laws. I believe it was this lack of real recognition of individual differences that was the rock on which psychology's early attempts to establish itself as an introspective discipline foundered. Following the lead of their more successful physicist and chemist colleagues, the early psychologists immediately began to look for the general Laws of the Mind, and then, when they found their data were not agreeing, they took to quarreling and wasted their energies. They tried too much to start with; they tried to abstract too much before coming to adequate terms with the prescribed subject matter.

We make the same mistake today all too often, albeit in a more "sophisticated" form. Suppose that in the course of an experiment we take a couple of measures on a group of subjects. For example, let measure X be the degree of analgesia the subject can show and let measure Y be the intensity of the subject's imagery. Tempted by the convenience and "scientificness" of a nearby computer, we dump our group data into a prepackaged analysis program and get a printout like that shown in the lower right-hand corner of Figure 8, showing a nice straight line fitted to the data and a highly significant (thus publishable) correlation coefficient between variables X and Y. It looks as if ability to experience analgesia is linearly related to intensity of imagery.

If we distrust this much abstraction from the data, we might ask our computer to print out a scatter plot of the raw data. Then we might see something like the plot in the lower left-hand corner of Figure 8, which reassures us that our fitted curve and correlation coefficient are quite adequate ways of presenting and understanding our results.

Suppose, however, that we actually go back to our subjects

and retest some of them repeatedly, do a time sample of their simultaneous abilities to experience analgesia and to image, and suppose we find that our subjects actually fell into three clear types, as shown in the upper half of Figure 8. Type A shows either a low degree of both analgesia and imagery, or a fair degree of analgesia and imagery, but nothing else. Type B show a low-to-fair degree of analgesia and imagery, or a very high degree of analgesia and imagery, but nothing else. Type C shows a high variability of degree of analgesia and imagery.

For subjects of Type C, the conclusion drawn from the group data of a linear relationship between intensity of imagery and intensity of analgesia was a valid conclusion. But how many type C subjects were included in our group? Subjects of Types A and B, on the other hand, do *not* show a linear relationship between X and Y, analgesia and imagery. For Type A subjects, X and Y cluster together at low levels of

FIGURE 8. Methodological Problems in Using Group Data.

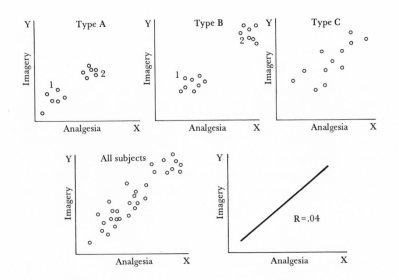

functioning or at moderate levels of functioning, but show no clear linear relationship within either cluster. For type B subjects, X and Y cluster at low-to-moderate or at very high levels, and again show no clear linear relationship within either clustering. Indeed, subjects of type A and B show the clustering we used to define the concept of d-SoCs, while subjects of type C seem to function in only a single d-SoC.

Note, too, that if we had a distribution of subjects mostly of types A and B, and only a few Cs in our experimental group, and if we average a single data point from each subject, and some of the As and Bs are in one or another of the d-SoCs they can be in, then we will get pseudocontinuity in our group data and not even suspect the existence of different d-SoCs in our experiment. We shall think all subjects are type C. There may even be more d-SoCs than is apparent at first glance, for while the lower clusters for type A and type B subjects might be the same d-SoC, the moderate and high ones might not be.

A variety of misinterpretations of experimental data can result from these types of errors.

I think it is hard to realize the full impact of these individual differences because of the deep (emotional) ingrained nature of the assumption that we all share a common state of consciousness to begin with, our ordinary or so-called "normal" state of consciousness. Insofar as we are members of a common culture this is generally true, but the more I have really gotten to know other individuals and started to get a feeling for the way their minds work, the more I have become convinced that this general truth, the label "ordinary state of consciousness," conceals enormous individual differences. If I clearly understood the way your mind works in its ordinary state, and vice versa, we would both be amazed. Yet because we speak a common language that stresses external events rather than internal ones, we are seldom aware of the differences.

Psychologically, we each tend to assume that our own mind

is an example of a "normal" mind, and we then project our own experiences onto other people without being aware of how much projecting we are doing. This can have interesting results scientifically. For example, there is a raging controversy in the hypnosis literature now over whether the concept of a d-SoC is necessary to explain hypnosis, or whether the hypnotic state is in fact continuous with the ordinary state, simply exhibits certain psychological functions, such as suggestibility and role-playing involvement, pushed to somewhat higher levels of activity than they are under ordinary conditions. One of the chief proponents of this latter view, Theodore X. Barber, is someone who can produce most of the classical hypnotic phenomena in himself without doing anything "special"; i.e., he can sit down and anesthetize his hand or produce mild hallucinations and the like without experiencing a breakdown of his ordinary consciousness, a transitional period, or anything else "special."[11] That is, the range of phenomena included in his ordinary state of consciousness encompasses experiences that, for another person, must be attained by unusual means.* How much does this affect his theorizing? To go back to Figure 8, whereas A- and B-type people might have one state of consciousness that we call their ordinary state and a second called their hypnotic state, type C's ordinary range of consciousness includes both of these regions. So it is more accurate to say that what has been called hypnosis, to stick with this example, is indeed "merely" an extension of the ordinary range of functioning for *some* people, but for other people it is a d-ASC.

I cannot emphasize too strongly that the mapping of experience and the use of the concept of d-SoCs *must first be done on an individual basis. Only* after that, *if* regions of great similarity across individuals are found, does it become

---

* As we shall discuss in the section on ego states, some individuals may transit so rapidly and easily between d-SoCs that they do not notice the transitions, and so mistakenly believe they experience only one state of consciousness.

legitimate to coin common names that apply across individuals.

Naturally this is an idealistic statement, and does not reflect the way it was done! The very fact that we have names like dreaming state or hypnotic state indicates that there appears to be a degree of commonality among a fair number of individuals, and I shall often speak as if this were true, but it is hard to say how far commonality goes with any precision at the present stage of our knowledge, and it is clearly misleading at times.

Induction of a Discrete
Altered State of Consciousness

Let us look at the process of inducing a d-ASC.

Our starting point is the base-line state of consciousness (b-SoC), usually our ordinary state of consciousness. The b-SoC is an active, stable, over-all patterning of psychological functions which, via multiple (feedback) stabilization relationships among the parts making it up, maintains its identity in spite of environmental changes. I emphasize *multiple* stabilization, for, like any well-engineered, complex system, there are many processes maintaining a state of consciousness: it would be too vulnerable to unadaptive disruption if there were only one or two stabilization processes.

Given this starting point, inducing the transition to a d-ASC is a three-step process, based on two psychological (and/or physiological) operations. I will describe the steps of the process sequentially and the operations sequentially, but realize that in reality the same action may function for both induction operations.

INDUCTION OPERATIONS

The first induction operation is to *disrupt* the stabilization of the b-SoC, to interfere with the loading, positive and negative feedback, and limiting processes and structures that keep the psychological structures operating within their ordinary range. We must disrupt several stabilization processes. For example, during a lecture I may clap my hands loudly, and, since the audience has been listening to me drone on for a while, the clap is somewhat startling, and certainly increases the level of activation of the audience and may even have made some jump. I doubt very much, however, that anyone would enter into a d-ASC, even though the level of activation for some listeners peaked up rather high momentarily. By throwing a totally unexpected and intense stimulus into an individual's mind, I caused a momentary shift *within* the pattern of his ordinary state of consciousness but not a shift to an altered state. If the person were a little drowsy I might have totally disrupted one or more stabilization processes for a moment, but since he has multiple stabilization processes going on, this was not sufficient to alter his state of consciousness.*

So the first operation in inducing a d-ASC is to disrupt enough of the multiple stabilization processes to a large enough extent that the base-line pattern of consciousness can no longer hold together. One may try to disrupt stabilization processes directly when they can be identified, or indirectly by pushing some psychological functions to and beyond their limits of functioning. One may disrupt particular subsystems, e.g., by overloading them with stimuli, depriving them of stimuli, or giving them anomalous stimuli which can't be processed in habitual ways. Or one may disrupt the functioning of a subsystem by withdrawing attention/awareness energy from it, a gentle kind of disruption. If the operation of our subsystem is disrupted it may alter the operation of a

---

* This particular example works for the ordinary state of consciousness, but if an individual were asleep he may have been awakened as a result of this particular loud stimulus. The clap might be sufficient in a sleep state to disrupt stabilization enough to allow a transition back to ordinary waking consciousness.

second subsystem via feedback paths, etc.

The second induction operation is to apply what I call *patterning forces*, stimuli that then push disrupted psychological functioning toward the new pattern of the desired d-ASC. These patterning stimuli may also serve to disrupt the ordinary functioning of the b-SoC insofar as they are incongruent with the functioning of the b-SoC. Thus the same stimuli may serve as both disruptive and patterning stimuli. For example showing someone a diagram that makes no sense or is unesthetic in the base-line state would be a mild disrupting force, but the same diagram might make sense or be esthetically pleasing in the desired altered state, and thus be a patterning force.

INDUCTION STEPS

Figure 9 sketches the steps of the induction process, using the analogy of d-SoCs as being like blocks, of various shapes and sizes (representing particular psychological structures), forming a system or construction (the state of consciousness) in a gravitational field (the environment). At the extreme left, we see a number of psychological structures assembled into a stable construction, our b-SoC. The detached figures below the construction represent some psychological potentials that are not available in the b-SoC.

The first figure on the left is our starting point, a stable state of consciousness. We begin applying disrupting (and patterning) forces to start induction. The second figure from the left is this beginning and represents *quantitative* change within the b-SoC, i.e., the disruptive (and patterning) forces are being applied, and while the over-all construction remains the same, some of the relationships within it have changed. Quantitative change has about reached its limit, as, for example, at the right and left end of the construction, things are close to falling apart. Particular psychological structures and subsystems have varied as far as they can while

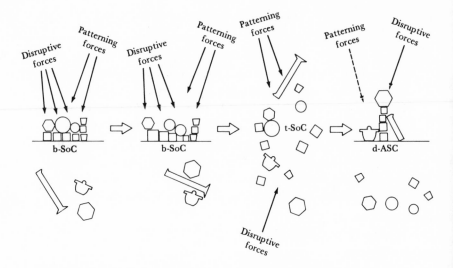

FIGURE 9. Induction of a Discrete Altered State of Consciousness.

still maintaining the over-all system.* I have also drawn in some of the latent potentials outside of consciousness changing their relationship, something we must postulate from this theory and our knowledge of the dynamic unconscious, but about which we have very little empirical data** at present.

If the disrupting forces are successful in finally breaking down the organization of the b-SoC, the second step of the induction process occurs, the construction or state of consciousness comes apart, and a transitional period occurs. In the figure this is represented by the parts of the construction being scattered about, with no clear-cut relationships to one another, or perhaps momentary relationships forming, as with the small square, the circle, and the hexagon on the left side of it. The disrupting forces are represented by the light arrow, as they are not as important now that the disruption

* There is a *depth* or intensity dimension within some d-SoCs, which I have discussed elsewhere.[12]
** Psychoanalytic studies[7] of hypnotic induction, e.g., give us inferential information on such activities.

has actually occurred, while the patterning forces are represented by the heavy arrows. The patterning stimuli must now push the isolated psychological structures into a new construction, the third and final step of the processes, where a new, self-stabilized structure, the d-ASC, forms. Some of the psychological structures or functions present in the b-SoC, such as those represented by the squares, trapezoids, circles, and small hexagon, may not be available in this new state of consciousness, while other psychological functions not available in the b-SoC may have now become available. Some functions available in the b-SoC may be available at the same or an altered level of functioning in the d-ASC.

I have also indicated that the patterning forces and disrupting forces may have to continue to be present, perhaps in attenuated form, in order for this new state to be stable; i.e., it may not have enough internal stabilization at first to hold up against internal or environmental change, and so artificial "props" are needed. A person, for example, may at first have to be hypnotized in a very quiet supportive environment in order to make the transition into hypnosis, but, after being hypnotized a few times, the d-ASC is stable enough so that he can be hypnotized under very noisy, chaotic conditions.

In following this example the reader probably thought of going from his or her ordinary state to some more exotic altered state of consciousness, but this theoretical sequence applies for transition from any d-SoC to any other d-SoC. Indeed, this is also the *de*induction process, the process of going from a d-ASC back to the b-SoC. Forces are applied to disrupt the altered state, and patterning forces to reinstate the base-line state; there is a transitional period; and the base-line state reforms. Since it is generally much easier to get back into our ordinary state, because it is so overlearned, than to get into an altered state, we usually pay little attention to the deinduction process, although it is just as complex in principle as the induction process.

We shall consider the question of what can be self-observed during the transitional period later.

It may be that some d-SoCs cannot be reached directly from another particular d-SoC, but some intermediary d-SoC has to be gone through. It would be like crossing a stream that is too wide to leap over directly, so that one or more stepping stones in sequence are needed to get to the other side. Each stepping stone is a stable place in itself, but they are transitional with respect to the beginning and end points of the process. Some of the *jnana* states of Buddhist meditation[13] may be of this nature. This kind of stable transitional *state* should not be confused with the inherently unstable transitional *periods* we have been talking about above.

FALLING ASLEEP

In the interest of brevity no adequate example of the induction process will be given here, but we will consider the highlights of the process of going to sleep. You lie down in a dim, quiet room, closing your eyes. Most of the loading stabilization of the external environment is thus removed. By lying still, your kinesthetic receptors adapt out, removing the loading stabilization input from your body. You adopt an attitude of nothing being particularly important—there's nothing to accomplish—so attention/awareness is withdrawn from both positive- and negative-feedback stabilization systems, as there's no "norm" to hold the system to. These are all gentle disrupting forces. Tiredness, the physiological need for sleep, is both a further disrupting force and a preprogrammed, "hardware" patterning force. As the data reported by Vogel et al. (discussed earlier) illustrate,[6] the intact ego state, the ordinary state of consciousness, persists for a time after lying down, then as reality contact and plausibility of thought are lost, the destructuralized ego state appears. We will take the destructuralized state as the transitional period, although future research may require us to make finer distinctions here if there turns out to be a stable pattern to this apparently destructuralized state. Then the transitional period ends with the restructuralized ego state, with plausibility of content returning even though reality contact remains lost. Vogel et al. accept a psychoanalytical interpretation of this, viewing the restructuring as due to defenses against the anxiety the destructuralized state could lead to. As defense mechanisms have temporarily broken down in the destructuralized state, we would say further patterning forces operate to form the restructuralized state, the d-ASC.

Methodological Hazards
of Operationalism

In our consideration of induction, we come to another major methodological pitfall that has greatly plagued psychological research on altered states. This is operationalism, carried out "rigorously," to the point of absurdity. That is, in our search for "objectivity" we start putting our emphasis on parameters that can be physically measured, to the point of making our experiments useless.

The primary example that comes to mind in psychological research is the equating of the hypnotic *state* with the *performance* of the hypnotic induction *procedure* by the hypnotist. The hypnotic *state* is a purely psychological construct (or experience if you've ever achieved it), not at all definable by measurement with a voltmeter or a camera. The hypnotic induction *procedure*, on the other hand, the "magic" words that the hypnotist says aloud, is susceptible to physical measurement. One can photograph it, videotape it, record it, measure the intensity of the hypnotist's voice, and come up with all sorts of precise physical measurements. If we now talk about the "hypnotized" subjects as some experimenters do, when we mean the subjects who sat in the same room while the hypnotist read the magic words (an objective measurement), we make a serious mistake, for the fact that the *hypnotist* goes through the procedure does not mean that the *subject* will enter the d-SoC we call hypnosis.

I stress that the concept of a d-ASC is a *psychological, experiential construct*, and so the ultimate criterion for whether a subject is in an altered state is a mapping of his experiences to determine at a given time whether he is actually in a region of psychological space we call a d-ASC.* We must not equate a d-ASC with the performance of the induction technique. Going through a hypnotic induction does not necessarily induce hypnosis, lying down in bed does not necessarily mean you're sleeping or dreaming, performing a meditation exercise does not necessarily mean that you enter into some kind of meditative state of consciousness.

Where the induction technique is apparently physiological, as, for example, using drugs, it is very tempting to think that using the method is always followed by the altered state, but even that is false. Smoking marijuana, e.g., does not necessarily mean that someone gets "stoned," enters into a discrete altered state. I shall elaborate on this below.

I do not mean to imply that in reporting experiments the description of techniques is unimportant—we certainly need to do that, but we also need to have measures of the *effectiveness* of these techniques in actually altering a state of consciousness *for each individual subject*.

In this chapter we shall not go into a discussion of how these assessments can be carried out, but I refer the reader to an article of mine on self-report scales for measuring the depth of altered states of consciousness,[12] and to another study carried out with E. Kvetensky on scaling the level of marijuana intoxication,[14] to show some of the ways we can do this.**

---

* Practically, once we have an adequate over-all map for a particular d-SoC for a given subject, we may just sample a few uniquely characteristic points to decide whether the subject is in that d-SoC at a given time.

** I shall not at this time treat physiological correlates of discrete states of consciousness, so I shall just mention that where we have such correlates

In discussing operationalism here, I have been referring to a *physical* operationalism, a system defined in terms of the manipulation of external, physical objects. Ultimately we need an *internal* operationalism to define crucial terms and processes in experience. Our present language is very poor for this, so we are a long way from the precision of an internal operationalism.

The Use of Drugs to Induce Discrete Altered States of Consciousness

I spoke of the methodological pitfall that comes from equating a *technique* that might *induce* a d-ASC with the altered state itself. This error is particularly seductive when one is talking about psychoactive or psychedelic drugs, for we tend to accept the pharmacological paradigm, the essence of which is that the specific chemical nature of the drug interacts with the chemical and physical structure of the nervous system in a lawfully determined way, invariably producing certain kinds of results. This view may be mostly true at neurological levels, but can be more misleading than helpful when dealing with consciousness. Observed variability in human reactions tends to be seen as the perverseness of psychological idiosyncrasies, interfering with basic physiological reactions, and averaged out by treating it as "error variance." While this pharmacological paradigm seems usefully valid for a variety of simple drugs, such as barbituates for inducing drowsiness and sleep, it is quite inadequate and misleading when one deals with the psychedelic drugs like marijuana or LSD.

(stage-1 REM dreaming, for example), fine, we can use them with the convergent operations strategy advocated by Stoyva and Kamiya,[15] but we must remember that state of *consciousness* is a psychological concept, and psychology does not need a physiological basis to be scientific and useful. Indeed, premature "physiologizing" has hampered the development of psychology.

NONDRUG FACTORS

Figure 10 shows a complete model of drug effects on consciousness that I developed when I was beginning to study marijuana intoxication.[16,17] In addition to the physiological factors, producing disrupting and patterning forces impinging on the subject, shown in the upper right side of the figure, there are a large number of psychological disrupting and patterning forces which, in many cases, are far more important for determining whether a d-ASC will occur and what the exact nature of that altered state will be than the physiological effects of the drug. Thus while it is useful to know what drug a subject has taken, the quantity of the drug, and the method of administration, in some ways these are among the least important components of the situation one can know. Without having some knowledge of the psychological factors, it may be very difficult to predict with any accuracy at all what the subject's behavioral and experiential reactions will be.

Just to briefly mention these nondrug factors, they include the culture in which a person was raised and all the effects the culture has had in terms of structuring his b-SoC and providing specific expectations about the drug; the particular personality of the subject; possible specific physiological vulnerabilities he might have to the drug; and particularly his learned drug skills: has he taken this drug many times before and learned to enhance desired reactions and inhibit undesired reactions, or is he naïve with respect to this drug, so that most of his energy will go into coping with the (often stressful) effects of novelty?

Then we come to a class of more immediate factors. What is the subject's mood when he takes the drug, since this mood may be amplified or inhibited? What does he expect to experience in this situation? Are these expectations the same as what he *desires* to experience?

Then there are other factors dealing with the situation or experimental setting in which the drug is taken. What is the

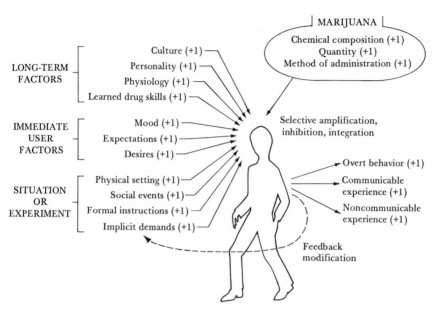

FIGURE 10. Drug-Induced Effects on Consciousness.

physical setting, and how does that affect the subject? And how about the social setting? What kind of people are with the subject and how do they interact with him? A frightened person present, for example, may communicate his fright sufficiently to the subject to make the effect of the drug quite anxiety provoking. If this is an experiment, what are the formal instructions given to the subject, and how does he react to and interpret them? Perhaps even more important, what are the demand characteristics,[18,19] the *implicit* instructions, and how do they affect the subject? If, for example, the experimenter tells the subject that the drug is relatively harmless, but has him sign a comprehensive medical release form, the total message communicated belies the statement that this is a relatively harmless drug.

Further, the subject is not a passive recipient of all these forces impinging on him, but may selectively facilitate the action of some of them and inhibit others. Again, we will not go into any detail on these many nondrug factors, but they are vitally important in determining how a drug will affect a person, whether or not a d-ASC will result from the drug's action, and the specific nature of events within that d-ASC.

PHYSIOLOGICAL AND
PSYCHOLOGICAL EFFECTS

Given this cautionary note on the complexity of using drugs to induce altered states of consciousness, there are nevertheless a few general things we can say about drug-induced states in terms of our theoretical model. Particular drugs may have specific effects on the neurological basis of various psychological structures/subsystems, possibly exciting or activating some of these structures/subsystems, suppressing or slowing the activity of others of these structures/subsystems, or altering or distorting the particular mode of information processing within some structures/subsystems. Psychological processes in relatively unaffected structures/subsystems may compensate for changes in affected subsystems and/or maintain sufficient stabilization processes so that the b-SoC does not break down. That is, the drug may both disrupt and pattern on a *physiological level*. How does this translate to a psychological level?

Given physiological effects that may affect various structures/subsystems, we must remember that it is how you *interpret* a particular physiological effect that determines much of your reaction to it and whether or not a d-ASC may result. To take one of the most common examples, most marijuana smokers have to *learn* how to achieve the d-ASC we refer to as marijuana intoxication or being "stoned." Typically, the first few times a person smokes marijuana, he may feel an occasional isolated effect, but the over-all pattern of his consciousness remains that of his ordinary state, and he usually wonders why people make so much fuss about taking a drug which doesn't seem to do much of anything interesting. With the assistance of more experienced drug users who suggest he focus his attention on certain kinds of happenings or try to have certain specified kinds of experiences, additional psychological factors, patterning and disrupting forces, are brought to bear to disrupt the ordinary state of consciousness and pattern the d-ASC. The transition takes place quite suddenly and the person finds that he is now stoned. This is a good illustration of how the physiological action of the marijuana may disrupt many of the ordinary stabilization processes of our ordinary state of consciousness but not enough of them, so the state of consciousness does not change.

The fact that naïve users may smoke enormous amounts of marijuana the first several times without getting stoned, and then easily get stoned with a tenth as much drug for the rest of their marijuana-use careers is paradoxical to pharmacologists. They have called this the "reverse tolerance effect." This effect is not at all puzzling in terms of our theoretical framework. It simply says that the disrupting and patterning effect of the drug per se is generally not sufficient to destabilize the base-line state of consciousness. Once the user knows how to deploy his attention/awareness properly, however, this deployment needs only a small amount of boost from the physiological effects of the drug to destabilize the base-line state and pattern the altered state of being stoned.

Indeed, the "placebo" response of getting stoned on marijuana that has had the THC extracted from it may not illustrate the idea that some people are fools so much as illustrating that psychological factors may be the main component of the altered state associated with marijuana use.

We should also note that it is common for marijuana users to say they can "come down" at will; i.e., if they find themselves in a situation that they don't feel able to cope with adequately while in the d-ASC of marijuana intoxication, they can deliberately suppress all the effects and temporarily return, almost instantly, to their ordinary state of consciousness.[17] By psychological methods they can disrupt the altered state and pattern their ordinary state into existence.

A third and quite striking example of the importance of psychological factors in determining whether a drug produces a d-ASC or not comes from a review by Snyder[20] of the attempts to use marijuana in medicine in the nineteenth century. Snyder says, "It is striking that so many of these medical reports fail to mention any intoxicating properties of the drug. Rarely, if ever, is there any indication that patients— hundreds of thousands must have received cannabis in Europe in the nineteenth century—were 'stoned,' or changed their attitudes toward work, love, their fellow men, or their homelands. . . . When people see their doctor about a specific malady, they expect a specific treatment and do not anticipate being 'turned on.' " Apparently then, unless you have the right kind of expectations and a "little help from your friends," it is unlikely that marijuana will produce a d-ASC, so equating the ingestion of marijuana with the existence of a d-ASC is a very tricky business.

One might think that this shows that marijuana is a weak drug, but it is also true that some people do not respond to large doses of far more powerful drugs like LSD.

MAJOR PSYCHEDELIC DRUGS

In dealing with the very powerful drugs like LSD, mescaline, or psilocybin, we come into an area of extreme variability of reactions that requires great caution. It is clear that for almost everyone who takes these more powerful psychedelic drugs, the ordinary state of consciousness is disrupted, and in a sense we may say that the *primary effect* of the powerful psychedelic drugs is the disruption of the stabilization processes of the ordinary state of consciousness, so that state breaks down. But, while there is a great deal of commonality of experience among marijuana users[17] (at least in our cultural setting), so that it is useful to speak of the "marijuana state" as a distinctive state of consciousness across subjects, variability with the powerful psychedelics is so great that I interpret present evidence as showing that there is no particular d-SoC necessarily produced by the major psychedelic drugs. Rather, we see a highly unstable state in which we never get more than very transient formations of patterns. The temporary association of scattered functions in the third part of Figure 9 illustrates this. We see continuous transition between various kinds of unstable states. The colloquial phrase "tripping" is very apropos; one is continually going somewhere but never arriving.

Now while this is probably true for most of the uses of powerful psychedelics in our culture, it is not universally true. In reading Carlos Castaneda's fascinating accounts of his work with don Juan[8,21,22] one realizes that Castaneda's initial reactions to psychedelic drugs were like this, but don Juan was not interested in his "tripping." Instead don Juan tried to train him to *stabilize* the effects of psychedelic drugs so that he could get into a particular d-SoC suited for a particular kind of task at various times. So it would seem that with the addition of further psychological patterning forces to the primarily disruptive forces caused by psychedelic drugs, it is possible that stable states of consciousness can be developed that will have particularly interesting properties.

Meanwhile, we should not use terms like "the LSD state," or believe that the statement "X took LSD" tells us much of anything about what has happened to X's consciousness.

Observation of
Internal States

Ordinarily when we think of observation in science we think of observing the external environment, and the observer is taken for granted. Or, if we recognize that the observer has inherent characteristics which limit his adequacy to observe, we simply attempt to compensate for these specific characteristics, as by aiding his senses with instruments, and again largely take the observer for granted—our interest being in the external phenomena. When we use experiential data in trying to understand states of consciousness, it becomes questionable to simply take the observer for granted; so let us look at the process of observation in more detail.

Given what has been said earlier about the construction of ordinary consciousness or of any d-SoC, making experiential observations about one's own state of consciousness requires that the system observe itself. Attention/awareness must activate structures which are capable of observing processes going on in other structures.

Now there seem to be two ways of doing this, which we shall discuss as if they were completely separate, even though in many actual instances they may be mixed. The first way is to see the d-SoC, the system, breaking down into two subsystems, one of which constitutes the observer and the other of which constitutes the system to be observed. I notice, for example, that I am rubbing my left foot as I write and that this action does not seem to be relevant to the points I want to make. A moment ago I was absorbed in the thinking involved in the writing and rubbing the foot, but some part of me then stepped back for a moment, under the impetus to find an example to illustrate the current point, and noticed that I was rubbing my foot. The "I" that observed that I was rubbing my foot is very much my ordinary I, my personality, my ordinary state of consciousness. The observation is that the major part of my system, my personality, my ordinary state of consciousness held together but temporarily singled out a small, connected part of itself to be observed. Insofar as I am still my ordinary "I," all the characteristics of that particular observation are my characteristics. Thus there is no "objectivity" to my own observation of myself. My ordinary "I," for example, is always concerned with whether what I am doing is useful for attaining my short-term and long-term goals, and the judgment was automatically made that the rubbing of the foot was a useless waste of energy. Having immediately classified foot rubbing as useless, I had no further interest in observing it more clearly, seeing what it was like.

By contrast, many meditative disciplines take the view that attention/awareness can achieve a very high degree of independence from the particular structures that constitute our ordinary state of consciousness and our personality, that is, that one possesses (or can develop) an Observer that is highly objective with respect to the ordinary personality because it is an Observer that is essentially pure attention/awareness—it has no characteristics of its own. If the Observer had been active, I might have observed that I was rubbing my foot, but there would have been no structure immediately activated that passed judgment on this action. Judgment, after all, means relatively permanent characteristics coded in structure to make comparisons against. The observer would simply have noted whatever was happening without judging it.

The existence of the Observer is an experiential reality to many people, especially those who have attempted to develop such an Observer by practicing meditative disciplines. We shall treat it as an experiential reality and not get involved in the question of its ultimate degree of separation from any kind of structure. It may depend on certain structures which have no connections with other structures, i.e., be an aware but dissociated subsystem, a discrete state of its own.

In many instances it would not be easy to make a clear-cut distinction between the observer and the Observer. Many times, for example, when I am attempting to function as an Observer, I will Observe myself doing certain things, but this Observation immediately activates some aspect of the structure of my ordinary personality which then acts as an observer connected with various value judgments which are then triggered. That is, I pass from the function of Observing from "outside" the system to observing from "inside" the system, from relatively objective observation to the judgmental observation by my conscience or superego. There are meditative disciplines which supposedly make one able to maintain the Observer for very long periods of time, with this Observer also able to Observe the judgments consequent upon observation by the ordinary observer.

The distinction between these two kinds of observer is important in considering the transition period between two d-SoCs. If we ask questions about what kinds of phenomena are experienced during the transition period, we must consider who is going to make these experiential observations for us? Insofar as our ordinary observer *is* the structure, the d-SoC, the b-SoC, the radical destructuring necessary for a transition into a d-ASC eliminates the ability to observe. At worst, if there is total destructuring, then we should expect no direct experiential observation of the transitional period at all, perhaps only a feeling of blankness. Some people do report this. This situation is often not that bad, however. Destructuring of the b-SoC may not be total, certain parts of it may hold together as subsystems through the transition period; partial observations may be made by these subsystems, and then the observations may be recoverable on return to the base-line state or in the d-ASC. But the observations are necessarily limited and incomplete; they come from a partially incapacitated observer.

Now consider the case of the Observer, *if* it is well developed in a particular person, during the transition from one d-SoC to another. Because the Observer is not at all based in particular structures, only partially based in particular structures, or based in structures that are not part of the b-SoC undergoing destructuring,* it should have a much greater capacity to observe transitional phenomena. We have exactly

* Hilgard[23] has found the concept of an, at least, partially dissociated observer useful in understanding hypnotic analgesia.

this sort of report of phenomena from some individuals who feel they have a fairly well-developed Observer. They feel that this Observer can make essentially continuous observations not only within a particular d-SoC but during the transition between two or more discrete states.

I shall say no more about the nature of the Observer at this time because we know so little about it in our Western scientific tradition, but I think it is clear that it is extremely important to find out to what extent the Observer's apparent objectivity is a reality and to what extent a fiction. Insofar as it is a reality, it offers a kind of objectivity and a possible escape from cultural consensus-reality conditionings which is highly important.

Discrete States of Consciousness and Identity States

The concept of d-SoCs comes to us in common-sense form, as well as out of my initial research interests, from the experience of *radically* altered states of consciousness, states like drunkenness, dreaming, marijuana intoxication, and certain meditative states. These represent such radical shifts in the patterning, the system properties of consciousness, that most observers experiencing them are *forced* to notice that the state of their consciousness is quite different.* That is, people need not have developed an Observer in order to notice such a change in their state of consciousness; a number of things are so clearly different that the observation is forced on them.**

---

* I say most observers to allow again for the fact of individual differences. Some people are extremely poor observers of their state of consciousness.

** The lack of full automatization of many functions in altered states also serves to make their "differentness" more noticeable. With continued experience of an altered state, automatization may rob it of its glamour and freshness. Chronic marijuana users, e.g., report fewer clear qualities of the state—this may be automatization in addition to, or instead of, any chemical tolerance build-up.

Although this is the origin and the main focus of the concept of d-SoCs, the theoretical approach we have discussed today is applicable to many variations occurring within the over-all pattern that we call our "ordinary" state of consciousness, variations which can be called ego states or *identity states*. Both my own self-observation and large amounts of psychological data, particularly data gathered in the course of psychoanalytic investigations, indicate that as different situations impinge on us and activate different emotional drives, quite distinct changes in the organization of our egos can take place. Certain drives become inhibited or activated and the psychological functions around them alter and form a whole new constellation. These alterations in functioning that I call identity states are also d-SoCs within the concepts put forward by this theory. Yet, they are almost never noticed as d-SoCs for several reasons.

First, because each of us has a large repertoire of these identity states, and we transit between one and another of them extremely readily, practically instantly, there are practically no lapses or transitional phenomena that would make us likely to notice the transition.

Second, all of these various identity states share very large amounts of psychological functioning (for example, speaking English, responding to the same proper name, wearing the same set of clothes, etc.), so the many structures held in common make it difficult to notice differences through ordinary observational activities.

Third, all of our ordinary range of identity states share in our culturally defined consensus reality. That is, although certain aspects of reality are emphasized by particular identity states, the culture as a whole has allowed a very wide variety of identity states in its definitions of "normal" consciousness and consensus reality. Within our cultural-consensus reality, for example, there are well-understood concepts, perceptions, and allowed behaviors concerned with being angry, being sad, feeling sexual desire, being afraid, etc.

Fourth, our *identification* is ordinarily very high, complete, with each of these identity states. That is, we project the feeling of "I" on to it (the sense of the identity subsystem function). Coupled with the culturally instilled need to believe that we are a single personality, we thus tend to gloss over distinctions. Thus we say *I* am angry, *I* am sad, etc., rather than saying a state of sadness has organized mental functioning differently from a state of anger.

Fifth, identity states in a very real sense are *driven* by needs, fears, attachments, defensive maneuvers, coping mechanisms, etc., so this highly involved quality of an identity state makes it unlikely that the person involved will be engaged in much self-observation.

Sixth, because many identity states have as a central focus emotional needs and drives that are only partially socially acceptable or are socially unacceptable, and given that people need to feel accepted, an individual may have many important reasons *not* to notice that he has discrete identity states. Thus when he is in an identity state which is socially "normal," being a good person, and the like, he may not be able to be aware of a different identity state that sometimes occurs when he hates his best friend. The two things don't go together, so automatized defense mechanisms prevent him from being aware of the one identity state while in the other identity state. Ordinarily it takes special psychotherapeutic techniques to make people aware of these contradictory feelings and identity states within themselves. Meditative practices designed to create the Observer also facilitate this sort of knowledge.

The development of an Observer can allow a person considerable access to observing different identity states, and an outside observer may often clearly infer different identity states, but a person who, himself, has not developed the Observer function very well may never notice the many transitions from one identity state to another. Thus what we call ordinary consciousness, or what a society values as "normal" consciousness, may actually consist of a large number of d-SoCs, here called identity states, but the over-all similarities between these identity states and the difficulties in observing them, for reasons discussed above, lead us to think of ordinary consciousness as a relatively unitary state.

Insofar as our interest is in *radically* altered discrete states like hypnosis or drunkenness, the concept of the ordinary state of consciousness as relatively unitary is useful. As the present theoretical scheme becomes more articulated, however, we shall need to begin dealing with these identity states which exist within the boundaries of the ordinary state of consciousness, and which probably also function within the boundaries of various d-ASCs.

In this paper, then, I shall continue to use the terms *discrete state of consciousness* or *discrete altered state of consciousness* to refer to the rather radical alterations like hypnosis or drunkenness that gave rise to the concept in the first place, and use the term identity state to indicate the finer division.

Ultracomplex
Subsystems and Systems

There are very interesting cases where one or more of the subsystems, acting as parts of the system, the d-SoC, are so complex that they can be viewed as d-SoCs in themselves, as well as components of a more complex system.

Current work on the different modes of functioning of the right and left hemispheres of the brain,[24] e.g., suggests that we have two quite distinct modes of consciousness often functioning simultaneously and with a fair degree of independence from one another. The left-hemisphere functioning is verbal, analytic, sequential, while the right-hemisphere functioning is nonverbal, Gestalt, simultaneous. So each half could be profitably looked at as a d-SoC within the theoretical framework we have been sharing. Yet they do interact, they do share many common brain/psychological structures, so they form a more complex system that makes up our ordinary state of consciousness. Experientially, we have had so much alternation of dominance between these two modes of functioning that transition is, by conscious standards, virtually instantaneous, easy, and it is not noticeable. Or with both modes functioning simultaneously but sharing common structures, there may be relatively smooth, continuous variations in degree of dominance of the two modes, rather than discrete transitions.

An initial look at the phenomenology of various d-ASCs suggests that some involve considerable shift in the dominance of left- or right-hemisphere functioning; this will be a particularly interesting dimension to investigate.

Other examples of subsystems being so complex as to warrant analysis as if they were d-SoCs themselves are extreme examples of dissociation, especially those examples we call multiple personality, and subconscious processes. In each case, however, these ultracomplex subsystems do function as components of a more complex system/state of consciousness.

In some instances where the ultracomplex subsystem dominates functioning and suppresses the functioning of other subsystems, it is useful to view it as a d-ASC. Multiple personality cases are a good example.

Stability and Growth

Implicit in the very act of mapping an individual's psychological experiences is the assumption of a reasonable degree of stability of the individual's structure and functioning over time. There would be no point in putting in a lot of effort to obtain a map if the map was going to need to be changed before we had time to make much use of it.

Ordinarily we assume that the personality of an individual,

or his or her ordinary state of consciousness, is reasonably stable over quite long periods of time, generally over a lifetime, once his basic personality has been formed in late adolescence. The major exceptions to this assumption are where individuals are exposed to severe, abnormal conditions, such as disasters, that may radically alter parts of their personality structure, or to psychotherapy and related psychological-growth techniques. Although the personality change from much psychotherapy is often considered rather small, leaving our former map of the individual's personality relatively useful, it can be quite large in some individuals.

Applying this possibility of large change to the concept of d-SoCs, it is possible that an individual might eventually learn to merge two d-SoCs into one. Perhaps it might be a matter of transferring some state-specific experiences and potentialities back into the ordinary state, so that eventually most or many state-specific experiences would be available in the ordinary state. The ordinary state, in turn, could undergo certain changes in its configuration. Or, by growth or therapeutic work at the extremes of functioning of two d-SoCs, they might gradually be brought closer together until experiences were possible all through the former "forbidden region."

We might also get a sort of pseudomerging of two d-SoCs. As an individual more and more frequently makes the transition between the two states, he may automate the transition process to the point where he no longer has any awareness of it, and/or efficient routes through the transition process are so thoroughly learned that the transition process takes almost no time or effort. In a particular instance, unless the individual were observing his whole patterning of functioning or an observer was assessing the whole pattern of functioning, a single state of consciousness might be assumed to exist simply because transitions were not noticed. This case would be like the rapid, automated transitions between identity states within our ordinary state of consciousness.

Insofar as a greater number of human potentials are available in two states as compared to one, we can see such merging or learning of rapid transitions as growth. Whether the individual or his culture would see it as growth would depend on cultural valuations of the added potentials and the individual's own intelligence in actual utilization of the two states. Having more potentials available is no guarantee that they will be used wisely.

Strategies in Studying
Discrete States of Consciousness

Let us briefly overview the strategies to be used in investigating various d-SoCs that follow from our conceptual model. These are idealistic, and subject to modification in practice, especially as we already have a lot of (poorly organized and of varying value) data collected without this framework.

First, I reemphasize that we start with the study of *individuals*, the first task being to map the experiential space of various individuals to see if their experiences do show the distinctive clusterings and patternings that constitute d-SoCs. For subjects who show this, we go on to the second step of more detailed individual investigation. For those who do not, we begin to carry out studies across individuals to ascertain why some individuals show various discrete states and others do not; in addition to recognizing the importance of individual differences, we must find out why they exist and what function they serve.

Second, we map the various d-SoCs of particular individuals *in detail*. What are the main features of each state? What induction procedures produce the state? What deinduction procedures cause an individual to transit out of it? What are the limits of stability of the state? What uses, advantages does the state have? What disadvantages or hazards? Are there depth dimensions to the state? How do we measure the depth?

What are the convenient marker phenomena of the state to rapidly tell when someone is in it? These are the kinds of questions we must ask.

With this background, we can then profitably ask questions about interindividual similarities of the various discrete states. Are they enough alike across individuals to warrant common names? If so, does this tell us mainly about cultural background similarities of the individuals studied, or something more fundamental about the nature of the human mind?

Finally we can do more microscopic studies of the nature of particular discrete states, the various structures/subsystems comprising them, etc. I put this sort of investigation at a late stage in order to avoid *premature reductionism*, for we have already had too much of that—"basic" studies of certain states concentrating on some particular detail before we have enough of a good, general picture of the state to know if that detail is important.

In the latter stages of this plan of investigation we shall have gotten beyond a mainly descriptive and classificatory level and into a predictive level, with considerable sharpening of our investigations.

Methodological
Consequences
of the Theory

Many methodological points have been discussed in the course of outlining the theory. I shall briefly summarize some of the major ones here to bring them together.

First, the emphasis on the (semi-)arbitrary, constructed nature of our ordinary state of consciousness makes clear the cultural biases built into it, and our need to search continually for and be aware of these limiting biases in order to make scientific progress.

Second, the importance of basic awareness, attention-directed awareness, and self-awareness, particularly as they act as a kind of energy for activating psychological structures, focuses the need for a better understanding of these relatively neglected topics in psychology.

Third, the importance of system qualities, Gestalt qualities arising out of the interaction of basic structures activated by attention/awareness energy, points out the desirability of comprehensive, over-all mapping of d-SoCs, lest premature reductionism waste too much of our investigative energies on details of the trivial.

Fourth, the possibilities of tapping and developing latent human potentials for our personal and cultural development are inherent in this theoretical framework, because fuller understanding and control of d-ASCs are the key to such development in many cases.

Fifth, although the theory is primarily at a descriptive and organizing stage, to fit our current needs, the possibilities for prediction within it will allow sharpening of our knowledge about the fundamental structures/subsystems comprising the human mind.

Sixth, the great importance of individual differences is stressed, since ignoring this can lead to very erroneous experimental procedures and interpretation about d-SoCs, such as those obscuring the existence of particular discrete states.

Seventh, the recognition that we are dealing with complex patterns and multiple stabilization processes maintaining the functional integrity of d-SoCs points up the limited value of studies which investigate only single variables or which mistakenly equate the performance of experimental operations with the actual attainment of a d-ASC.

Eighth, the theory shows how too much dependence on the "pharmacological paradigm," the belief that the chemical nature of an ingested drug causes relatively invariant results due to physiological specificity, can result in misleading data when dealing with consciousness. The apparent paradox of "reverse tolerance" to marijuana, e.g., is not at all paradoxical within our conceptual framework as it follows naturally from the existence of multiple stabilization processes.

The final major methodological consequence, the need for state-specific sciences, deserves fuller discussion as it has been barely mentioned in the preceding parts of this chapter.

State-Specific Sciences

The theory of d-SoCs presented here is the background for a proposal I made several years ago in *Science*[25,26], a proposal for the establishment of *state-specific sciences*. Earlier in this chapter I pointed out that in many ways our ordinary state of consciousness is the product of an *arbitrary* way of constructing a state of consciousness, containing large numbers of structures shaped by our particular culture's value judgments. Our d-SoC could have been structured in a different form. Similarly any d-ASC is also a structure that is at least partially quite arbitrary in its construction.

Let me qualify the word arbitrary. Given that we have a real, physical world around us that we, as biological entities, have to survive in, there are limits to our arbitrariness in constructing a state of consciousness. If we walk off the edge of a cliff, we shall fall and be severely injured or killed. Any state of consciousness we can construct, any culturally determined consensus reality, will be *effective* in insuring biological survival from this particular peril if it provides some kind of structure/rationale to prevent us from walking off cliffs. We could construct one rationale based on a potent and invisible force called "gravity," which will throw one to the bottom and cause physical pain. Or we could construct a rationale based on the idea that demons lurk at the bottom of every cliff and smash up people who fall down. Or we could form a rationale around the belief that the rapid acceleration in falling makes the soul leave the body, thereby making the body vulnerable to physical hurt. Any of these structures encourages one not to step off the edge of cliffs.

Now it is very easy to think "But *our* reason is scientific!" Here we commit the all too common human fallacy of getting into shouting "*My* culture is better than your culture!" This interchange tends to continue with statements like "Well, if you don't believe my culture is better than yours, you pick up your spear and I'll pick up my hydrogen bomb and we'll see whose is better." I don't want to get into that level. It's a very big world we live in, and while we have some sciences that are very successful in *some* areas, we have not been terribly successful in others, especially psychological areas. The sheer size and complexity of the world we live in allow us to conceptualize it in a vast variety of ways—thus the diversity of cultures—and most of those ways are much too complex to be subjected to simple tests like whether or not you fall when you step over the edge of a cliff.

The science we have developed is an ordinary state-of-consciousness science; it is observation and conceptualization carried out within the highly selective framework provided by our culturally determined ordinary state of consciousness. This makes our science in many ways culture bound. We seem to have overcome a good deal of this "culture boundness" in the physical sciences: physical bodies fall at the same real rate (we firmly believe) regardless of the language of the observer who is measuring them. But in the psychological sciences, our observations and theories are very much culture bound, very much affected by our ordinary state of consciousness.

The intriguing methodological promise of d-ASCs is this: because d-ASCs constitute radically different ways of organizing our observations and conceptualizations of the universe, including ourselves, if we go ahead and develop a science *within* a particular d-ASC, we will have a quite different view of the universe. Insofar as one is careful to practice the essence of scientific method, as I have argued elsewhere,[25,26] the science developed in a particular discrete altered state will be just as scientific as our ordinary state-of-consciousness science. In some ways it would have the same kind of inherent blinders built in as ordinary state-of-consciousness science does, because, again, a d-ASC is still a partially arbitrary way of organizing consciousness. But by giving us a *different* look at things, a different perspective, it might greatly supplement or complement our ordinary consciousness science. The prospects are very intriguing, and I have dealt with them in detail in the original proposal.

Because I am a scientist my concern is with developing sciences operating within d-ASCs, but the hope that this sort of thing might be advantageous is hardly confined to scientists. One of the reasons so many of our children and students are using psychedelic drugs or meditating or practicing yoga and various other spiritual disciplines is that they have accepted the idea that our ordinary state of consciousness imposes certain dangerous limitations on us, and they believe that learning to function in various d-ASCs may organize their minds in ways that will at least partially by-pass some of those limits. It is easy to feel frustrated at the limits of our ordinary state of consciousness, and easy to become too enthusiastic about some of the obvious benefits of the view gained in d-ASCs, but most of our d-ASC enthusiasts have not yet learned that the partially arbitrary nature of altered states also gives *them* limitations. Everything has its price. I hope that the development of state-specific sciences will make both the advantages and the limitations of various d-ASCs clear to us soon, so that we may choose states appropriate to problems before we, as a culture or as individuals, enthusiastically exchange one set of limits for another, while shouting "Freedom!"

Summary

This paper presents a theoretical framework for understanding some aspects of human consciousness, particularly the areas called *states of consciousness* and *altered states of consciousness*. The theory casts light on a variety of areas, such as psychedelic drug use, which are not being treated well by conventional approaches.

We begin by noting that our ordinary state of consciousness is not something natural or just given but a highly complex *construction*, a specialized tool for coping with the environment and with each other, a tool that is useful for some things but not very useful for others. Sixteen basic theoretical postulates, based on human experience, cover the materials from which a state of consciousness is constructed.

The basic postulates start our theorizing with the existence of a basic *awareness*, and a more refined awareness of being aware, *self-awareness*. Because some volitional control of the focus of awareness is possible, it is referred to as *attention/ awareness*.

Further basic postulates deal with *structures*, those relatively permanent structures/functions/subsystems of the mind/brain which act on information to transform it in various ways. Arithmetical skills, e.g., constitute a structure, or a set of related structures. The structures of particular interest to us are those which require some amount of attention/ awareness to activate them. Attention/awareness acts like a *psychological energy* in this sense. Most systems for controlling the mind can be considered as ways of deploying attention/awareness energy so as to activate desirable structures (traits, skills, attitudes, etc.) and deactivate undesirable structures.

Psychological structures have individual characteristics which limit and shape the ways in which they can interact with one another. Thus, in considering systems built of psychological structures, the possibilities of the system are shaped and limited by both the deployment of attention/ awareness energy and the characteristics of the structures comprising the system. The human bio-computer, in other words, has a large, but limited number of possible modes of functioning.

Because we are born as human beings, creatures with a certain kind of body and nervous system operating on spaceship earth, a very large number of human potentialities are in principle available to us. But we are born into a particular culture which selects and develops a small number of these potentialities, actively rejects others, and is ignorant of most. The small number of experiential potentialities selected by our culture, and by some random factors, constitute the structural elements from which our ordinary state of consciousness is constructed. We are at once the beneficiaries and the victims of our culture's selectivity. The possibility of tapping and developing latent potentials outside the cultural norm by going into an altered state of consciousness, by temporarily restructuring our consciousness, is the basis of the great interest in this area.

The terms state of consciousness and altered state of consciousness have been used, too loosely, to mean whatever is on one's mind at the moment. The new term *discrete state of consciousness* (d-SoC) is proposed for scientific use. *A d-SoC is a unique, dynamic pattern or configuration of psychological structures, a d-SoC is an active system of psychological subsystems.* Although the component structures/subsystems show variation within a d-SoC, the over-all pattern, the over-all *system properties* remain recognizably the same. In spite of subsystem variation and environmental variation, a d-SoC is stabilized by a number of processes so it retains its identity and function. By analogy, an automobile remains an automobile whether on a road or in a garage (environment change), whether you change the brand of spark plugs or the color of the seat covers (internal variation).

Examples of d-SoCs are our ordinary waking state, non-dreaming sleep, dreaming sleep, hypnosis, alcohol intoxication, marijuana intoxication, and some meditative states.

A *discrete altered state of consciousness* (d-ASC) refers to a different d-SoC than some base-line state of consciousness. Usually our ordinary state is taken as the base-line state.

A d-SoC is stabilized by four kinds of processes: (1) *loading stabilization*, keeping attention/awareness energy deployed in habitual, desired structures by loading the person's system heavily with appropriate tasks; (2) *negative-feedback stabilization*, actively correcting the functioning of erring structures/subsystems when they deviate too far from the normative range that insures stability; (3) *positive-feedback stabilization*, providing rewarding experiences when structures/subsystems are functioning within desired limits; and (4) *limiting stabilization*, limiting the ability to function of structures/subsystems whose operation would destabilize the system.

In terms of current psychological knowledge, ten major subsystems (collections of related structures) which show important variations over known d-ASCs need to be distinguished, viz: (1) *Exteroceptors* (sense organs for sensing the external environment); (2) *Interoceptors* (senses for knowing what our bodies are feeling and doing); (3) *Input processing* (automated selecting and abstracting of sensory input so we perceive only what's "important" by personal and cultural consensus-reality standards); (4) *Memory*; (5) *Subconscious* (the classical Freudian unconscious plus many other psychological processes going on outside of our ordinary d-SoC, but which may become directly conscious in various d-ASCs); (6) *Emotions*; (7) *Evaluation and decision making* (our cognitive, evaluating skills and habits); (8) *Time sense* (the construction of *psychological* time and the placing of events within it); (9) *Sense of identity* (the quality added to experience that makes it *my* experience instead of "just" information); and (10) *Motor output* (muscular and glandular outputs to the external world and the body). These subsystems are not any sort of ultimates, but convenient categories to organize current knowledge.

Our present knowledge of human consciousness and d-SoCs is highly fragmented and chaotic. The main purpose of the proposed theory is organizational, as it collects and relates many formerly disparate bits of data, as well as having numerous methodological implications for guiding future research. It makes the general prediction that the number of stable d-SoCs available to humans is definitely limited (although we have not come anywhere near understanding those limits). It further provides a paradigm for making more specific predictions which will sharpen our knowledge about the structures and subsystems that make up human consciousness.

The theory stresses the importance of studying d-SoCs in one individual at a time because of enormously important *individual differences*. If we map the experiential space two people function in, one person may show two discrete, separated clusters of experiential functioning, two d-SoCs, while the other may show continuous functioning throughout both regions and the connecting regions of experiential space. The first must make a special effort to transit from one region of experiential space, one d-SoC, to the other; the second makes no such effort and does not experience the contrast of pattern and structure differences associated with the two regions, the two d-SoCs. So what is a "special" state of consciousness for one person may be an everyday experience for another. Great experimental confusion results if we do not watch for these differences. Unfortunately, many widely used experimental procedures are not sensitive to these important individual differences.

Induction of a d-ASC involves two basic operations which, if successful, lead to the d-ASC from the base-line state. First we apply *disrupting forces* to the base-line state, psychological or physiological or drug actions which disrupt the stabilization processes discussed above, either by interfering with them or by withdrawing attention-awareness energy from them. Because a d-SoC is a very complex system, with *multiple* stabilization processes operating simultaneously, induction may not work. A psychedelic drug, e.g., may not make a person enter a d-ASC because psychological stabilization processes hold the base-line state stable in spite of the disrupting action of the drug on a physiological level.

If induction is proceeding successfully, the disrupting forces push various structure/subsystems to their limits of stable functioning and then beyond, destroying the integrity of the system, disrupting the base-line d-SoC. Now *patterning forces* are applied during this transitional, disorganized period, psychological or physiological or drug actions which pattern structure/subsystems into a new system, the desired d-ASC. The new system, the d-ASC must develop its own stabilization processes if it is to last.

Deinduction, return to the base-line d-SoC, is the same process as induction. The d-ASC is disrupted, a transitional period occurs, the base-line d-SoC is reconstructed by patterning forces.

Psychedelic drugs like marijuana or LSD do not have invariant psychological effects, even though much misguided research assumes they do. Within the context of the present theory, such drugs are seen as disrupting and patterning forces whose effects take place in addition to other psychological factors, all mediated by the operating d-SoC. Consider the so-called "reverse-tolerance effect" with marijuana, where new users consume very large quantities of the drug at first with no feeling of being "stoned," i.e., in a d-ASC, then start using much smaller quantities regularly to get into the d-ASC of being stoned. It is not paradoxical in this framework, even though it is paradoxical from the standard pharmacological approach. The physiological action of the marijuana is not sufficient to disrupt the ordinary d-SoC until psychological factors also disrupt enough of the stabilization processes of the base-line d-SoC to allow transition to the d-ASC. These psychological forces are usually "a little help from my friends," the instructions for deployment of attention/awareness energy given by experienced users who know what functioning in the d-ASC of marijuana intoxication is like. These instructions also serve as patterning forces to shape the configuration of the d-ASC, to teach the new user how to *use* the physiological effects of the drug to form a new system of consciousness.

Shifts in research strategies that this theory calls for and methodological problems in research are discussed from the point of view of this theory, such as the way in which experiential observations of consciousness and transitions from one d-SoC to another are made. The theoretical framework can be applied within our ordinary d-SoC to deal with *identity states*, those rapid shifts in the central core of our identity and concerns which we overlook for many reasons, such as unacceptability of contradictions in ourselves, but which negatively influence so much of our daily life. Similarly the theoretical framework indicates that latent human potentialities may be developable and usable in various d-ASCs, so that learning to shift into the d-ASC *appropriate* for dealing with a particular problem may be seen as psychological growth. At the opposite extreme, certain kinds of psychopathology, such as multiple personality, can be treated as d-ASCs.

One of the most important consequences of the theory is the deduction that we need to develop *state-specific sciences*. Insofar as any particular d-SoC, whether a culture calls it "normal" or not, is a semiarbitrary way of structuring consciousness, a way that loses some human potentials while developing others, the sciences we have developed are one state-of-consciousness sciences. They are limited in some important ways. Our sciences have been very successful in dealing with the physical world, but not very successful in dealing with particularly *human* problems, psychological problems. If we applied scientific method to developing sciences *within* various d-ASCs, we would have sciences based on radically different perceptions, logics, communications, and so gain new views complementary to our current ones.

The search for new views, new ways of coping, through the experience of d-ASCs is hardly limited to science: it is a major basis for our culture's romance with drugs, meditation, Eastern religions, and the like. But infatuation with a new view, a new d-SoC, tends to make us forget that *any* d-SoC is a *limited* construction; there is a price to be paid for everything we get. It is vital for us to develop *sciences* of this powerful, life-changing area of d-ASCs if we are to optimize benefits from people's growing use of them and avoid the dangers of ignorant or superstitious tampering with the basic structure of our consciousness.

References

1. Can Consciousness Make a Difference?

1. Harman, Willis. "The new Copernican revolution." Unpublished paper.
2. LeShan, Lawrence. *Toward a General Theory of the Paranormal.* New York Parapsychology Foundation, December 1972, p. 12.
3. Ibid., pp. 81–82.
4. Wheeler, J. A. Interview. *Intellectual Digest,* June 1973, p. 32.
5. Castaneda, Carlos. "A tale of power." *Harper's Magazine.* September 1974, 249: 45. Article adapted from *Tales of Power.* New York: Simon and Schuster, 1974.
6. James, William. "The stream of consciousness." In *The Principles of Psychology, I.* New York: Dover Publications, 1950, pp. 224–290.
7. Ornstein, Robert E. *The Psychology of Consciousness.* San Francisco: W. H. Freeman, 1972, p. 182. Also New York: The Viking Press, 1973.
8. Brown, Barbara. "New mind, new body." Condensation in *Psychology Today,* August 1974, p. 94.
9. Sobel, David S. "Gravity and structural integration." In R. E. Ornstein, ed., *The Nature of Human Consciousness.* San Francisco: W. H. Freeman, 1973, pp. 397–407. Also New York: The Viking Press, 1974.
10. Farson, Richard E. President's letter, Esalen Catalog XI: 3, July–September 1974.
11. Ehrenreich, Barbara, and English, Deirdre. *Complaints and Disorders: The Sexual Politics of Sickness.* Old Westbury, N.Y.: The Feminist Press, 1973, p. 35.

12. Sobel, David S. "Gravity and structural integration." In R. E. Ornstein, ed., *The Nature of Human Consciousness*. San Francisco: W. H. Freeman, 1973, p. 407. Also New York: The Viking Press, 1974.

13. Wise, Harold, Grossman, Richard, Schwartz, Leni. The Center for Holistic Medicine, A Proposal. July 1, 1974.

14. Michaelson, M. G. "Death as a friendly onion." *New York Times Book Review*, July 21, 1974.

15. Erhard, Werner. Personal communication, 1974.

16. Shah, Idries. *Caravan of Dreams*. Baltimore: Penguin Books, 1972, p. 206.

17. Luria, S. E. "What can biologists solve?" *New York Review of Books*, February 7, 1974, p. 28.

18. Rogers, Carl R. "A humanistic conception of man." In R. E. Farson, *Science and Human Affairs*, Palo Alto: Calif., Science and Behavior Books, 1965, p. 23.

19. Shah, Idries, *Caravan of Dreams*. Baltimore: Penguin Books, 1972, p. 192.

2. A Science of Consciousness

1. Bruner, J. "On perceptual readiness." *Psychological Review*, 1957, 64: 123–152.

2. Ittelson, W. H., and Kilpatrick, F. P. "Experiment in perception." *Scientific American*, August 1951. Reprinted in Robert E. Ornstein, ed., *The Nature of Human Consciousness*. San Francisco: W. H. Freeman, 1973. Also New York: The Viking Press, 1974.

3. Festinger, L., Ono, H., Burnham, C. A., and Bamber, D. "Efference and the conscious experience of perception." *Journal of Experimental Psychology*, 1967, 74: 1–36.

4. Pribram, K. H. "The neurophysiology of remembering." *Scientific American*, January 1969, 73–86. Spinelli, D. N., and Pribram, K. H. "Changes in visual recovery functions and unit activity produced by frontal and temporal cortex stimulation." *Encephalography and Clinical Neurophysiology*, 1967, 22: 143–149.

5. Sperry, Roger. "Neurology and the mind-brain problem." *American Scientist*, 1951, 40: 291–312.

6. Bogen, J. E. "The other side of the brain." *Bulletin of the Los Angeles Neurological Society*, 1969, 34: I, 73–105; II, 135–162; III, 191–220. Reprinted in part in Robert E. Ornstein, ed., *The Nature of Human Consciousness*. San Francisco: W. H. Freeman, 1973. Also New York: The Viking Press, 1974.

3. The Two Modes of Consciousness and the Two Halves of the Brain

1. Shah, Idries. *Caravan of Dreams*. Baltimore: Penguin Books, 1972.
2. Shah, Idries. *The Exploits of the Incomparable Mulla Nasrudin*. New York: Dutton, 1972.
3. Polanyi, M. *Personal Knowledge*. New York: Harper & Row, 1958.
4. Sperry, R. W. "Hemisphere deconnection and unity in conscious awareness." *American Psychologist*, 1968, 23: 723–733.
5. Bogen, J. E. "The other side of the brain I. Dysgraphia and dyscopia following cerebral commissurotomy." *Bulletin of the Los Angeles Neurological Society*, 1969, 34: 73–105.
6. Bogen, J. E. "The other side of the brain II. An appositional mind." *Bulletin of the Los Angeles Neurological Society*, 1969, 34: 135–162.
7. Bogen, J. E. Final panel (part IV). In W. L. Smith ed., *Drugs and Cerebral Function*. Cerebral Function Symposium, Springfield, Ill.: Thomas, 1971.
8. Galin, D. "Implications for psychiatry of left and right cerebral specialization." *Archives of General Psychiatry*, 1974, 31: 572–583.
9. Levy, J. Trevarthen, C. Sperry, R. W. "Perception of bilateral chimeric figures following hemispheric deconnexion." *Brain*, 1972, 95: 61–78.
10. Galin, D., and Ornstein, R. "Lateral specialization of cognitive mode: An EEG study." *Psychophysiology*, 1972, 9: 412–418.
11. Bogen, J. E., and Bogen, G. M. "The other side of the brain III. The corpus callosum and creativity." *Bulletin of the Los Angeles Neurological Society*, 1969, 34: 191–220.
12. Gazzaniga, M. S. "Changing hemisphere dominance by changing reward probability in split-brain monkeys." *Experimental Neurology*, 1971, 33: 412–419.
13. Critchley, M. *The Parietal Lobes*. London: Arnold, 1953.

4. Physiological Studies of Consciousness

1. Levy, Jerre. "Possible basis for the evolution of lateral specialization of the human brain." *Nature*, 1969, 224: 614–615.
2. Lansdell, H. "Verbal and non-verbal factors in right hemisphere speech." *Journal of Comparative and Physiological Psychology*, 1969, 69: 734–738.
3. Galin, D., and Ornstein, R. "Lateral specialization of cognitive mode: An EEG study." *Psychophysiology*, 1972, 9(4): 412–418.
4. Doyle, J. C., Ornstein, R., and Galin, D. "Lateral specialization of

180 / *References*

cognitive mode: II. EEG frequency analysis." *Psychophysiology*, 1974, 11(5): 567–578.
5. Cohen, R. A. "Conceptual styles, culture conflict and non-verbal tests of intelligence." *American Anthropologist*, 1969, 71: 826–856.
6. Marsh, F. F., TenHouten, W. D., and Bogen, J. E. "A theory of cognitive functioning and social stratification." Progress Report, OEO contract. Dept. of Sociology, University of California, Riverside, 1970.

5. Bimodal Consciousness and the Mystic Experience

1. Laski, M. *Ecstasy: A Study of Some Secular and Religious Experiences.* London: Cresset Press, 1961.
2. James, William. *The Varieties of Religious Experience.* New York: Modern Library, 1929.
3. Ibid., p. 382.
4. Bucke, Richard M. *Cosmic Consciousness.* New York: University Books, 1961, p. 8.
5. Poulain, Augustine. *The Graces of Interior Prayer: A Treatise on Mystical Theology.* St. Louis: Herder, 1950, p. 272.
6. Lomax, Daniel (translator). "Heart of perfect wisdom sutra." *Omen,* 1971, 1(2): 25–26.
7. Deikman, Arthur J. "Experimental meditation." *Journal of Nervous Mental Diseases,* 1963, 136: 329–343.
8. Deikman, Arthur J. "Implications of experimentally induced contemplative meditation." *Journal of Nervous Mental Diseases,* 1966, 142: 101–116.
9. Hartmann, Heinz. *Ego Psychology and the Problem of Adaptation.* New York: International Universities Press, 1958, pp. 88–91.
10. Gill, Merton M., and Brenman, Margaret. *Hypnosis and Related States: Psychonalytic Studies in Regression.* New York: International Universities Press, 1959, p. 178.
11. Werner, Heinz. *Comparative Psychology of Mental Development.* New York: International Universities Press, 1957, p. 152.
12. Deikman, Arthur J. "De-Automatization and the mystic experience." *Psychiatry,* 1966, 29(4): 331.
13. Hilton, Walter. *The Scale of Perfection.* London: Burnes & Coates, 1953, pp. 14–15.
14. Suzuki, Shunryu. Lecture given at Zen Mountain Center, July 1968. *Wind Bell,* 1968, 7: 28.
15. Piaget, J. *The Construction of Reality in the Child.* New York: Basic Books, 1954.

16. Buber, M. *I and Thou*. New York: Charles Scribner's Sons, 1958.
17. Deikman, Arthur J. "Bimodal consciousness." *Archives of General Psychiatry*, 1971, 45: 483.
18. LeShan, Lawrence. "Physicists and mystics: similarities in world views." *Journal of Transpersonal Psychology*, 1969, 1(2): 1–20.
19. Bohr, Niels. *Essays, 1958–1962, on Atomic Physics and Human Knowledge*. New York: John Wiley, 1963.

6. Discrete States of Consciousness

1. Tart, C. *States of Consciousness*. New York: Dutton, 1975.
2. Tart, C. (ed.). *Transpersonal Psychologies*. New York: Harper & Row, 1975.
3. Tart, C. (ed.). *Altered States of Consciousness: A Book of Readings*. New York: John Wiley, 1969. Second edition, New York: Doubleday, 1972.
4. Van Eeden, F. "A study of dreams." *Proceedings of the Society for Psychical Research*, 1913, 26: 431–461. Reprinted in C. Tart, ed., *Altered States of Consciousness: A Book of Readings*. New York: John Wiley, 1969, pp. 145–158.
5. Tart, C., and Fridgen, J. "The transition from ordinary consciousness to being intoxicated with marijuana." In preparation.
6. Gill, M., and Brenman, M. *Hypnosis and Related States: Psychoanalytic Studies in Regression*. New York: International Universities Press, 1959.
7. Vogel, G., Foulkes, D., and Trossman, H. "Ego functions and dreaming during sleep onset." *Archives of General Psychiatry*, 1966, 14: 238–248. Reprinted in C. Tart, ed., *Altered States of Consciousness: A Book of Readings*. New York: John Wiley, 1969, pp. 75–92.
8. Castaneda, C. *A Separate Reality: Further Conversations with don Juan*. New York: Simon and Schuster, 1971.
9. Deikman, A. J. "De-automatization and the mystic experience." *Psychiatry*, 1966, 29: 329–343.
10. Ornstein, R. *On the Experience of Time*. Baltimore: Penguin Books, 1969.
11. Barber, T. X. "Suggested ('hypnotic') behavior: the trance paradigm versus an alternative paradigm." In E. Fromm and R. Shor, eds., *Hypnosis: Research Developments and Perspectives*. Chicago: Aldine/Atherton, 1972: pp. 115–183.
12. Tart, C. "Measuring the depth of an altered state of consciousness, with particular reference to self-report scales of hypnotic depth." In E. Fromm and R. Shor, eds., *Hypnosis: Research Developments and Perspectives*. Chicago: Aldine/Atherton, 1972, pp. 445–490.

13. Goleman, D. "The Buddha on meditation and states of consciousness, Part I." *Journal of Transpersonal Psychology*, 1972, 4: 1–44.
14. Tart, C., and Kvetensky, E. "Marijuana intoxication: feasibility of experiential scaling of level." *Journal of Altered States of Consciousness*, 1973, 1: 15–21.
15. Stoyva, J., and Kamiya, J. "Electrophysiological studies of dreaming as the prototype of a new strategy in the study of consciousness." *Psychological Review*, 1968, 75: 192–205.
16. Tart, C. "Marijuana intoxication: common experiences." *Nature*, 1970, 226: 701–704.
17. Tart, C. *On Being Stoned: A Psychological Study of Marijuana Intoxication*. Palo Alto, Calif.: Science and Behavior Books, 1971.
18. Orne, M. "On the social psychology of the psychological experiment, with particular reference to demand characteristics and their implications." *American Psychologist*, 1962, 118: 1097–1103.
19. Rosenthal, R. *Experimenter Effects in Behavioral Research*. New York: Appleton-Century-Crofts, 1966.
20. Snyder, S. *Uses of Marijuana*. New York: Oxford University Press, 1971.
21. Castaneda, C. *The Teachings of don Juan: A Yaqui Way of Knowledge*. Berkeley: University of California Press, 1968.
22. Castaneda, C. *Journey to Ixtlan: The Lessons of Don Juan*. New York: Simon and Schuster, 1972.
23. Hilgard, E. R. "A neodissociation interpretation of pain reduction in hypnosis." *Psychological Review*, 1973, 80: 396–411.
24. Ornstein, R. *The Psychology of Consciousness*. San Francisco: W. H. Freeman, 1972. Also New York: The Viking Press, 1972.
25. Tart, C. "States of consciousness and state-specific sciences." *Science*, 1972, 176: 1203–1210.
26. Tart, C. "Scientific foundations for the study of altered states of consciousness." *Journal of Transpersonal Psychology*, 1972, 3: 93–124.